BEST FOOD IN TOWN

BEST FOOD IN TOWN

The Restaurant Lover's Guide to Comfort Food in the Midwest

DAWN SIMONDS

emmis books

For further information, contact the publisher at

Emmis Books
1700 Madison Road
Cincinnati, OH 45206

www.emmisbooks.com

ISBN 1-57860-146-0

Library of Congress Cataloging-in-Publication Data

Simonds, Dawn, 1969-
Best food in town : the restaurant lover's guide to Midwest comfort food / by Dawn Simonds.
p. cm.
ISBN 1-57860-146-0
1. Restaurants--Middle West--Guidebooks.
2. Cookery, American--Midwestern style. 3. Comfort food. I. Title.
TX907.3.M55S56 2004
647.9577--dc22

2004053237

Cover designed by Stephen Sullivan
Interior designed by Susan Young
Edited by Jack Heffron and Jessica Yerega

For my family.

Acknowledgements

I'm grateful to Emmis Books for the opportunity to research and write this book. Without editor Jack Heffron and publisher Richard Hunt, I would not have come to know Midwest cuisine so well. My thanks to the chefs, owners, and restaurant workers of the restaurants in this book. Their work is the story. It is a privilege to convey it. I am also indebted to my fellow restaurant critics in the Midwest who offered opinions and advice; this book is better for their help, especially Mary Bergin of the Madison, Wisconsin *Capital Times*, Saimi Bergmann of the *Canton Repository* in Ohio, Jayne Bullock of the *Ames Tribune* in Iowa, Julie Failla Earhart in St. Louis, Brad Flory of the Michigan *Jackson Citizen Patriot*, Kathy Gibbons of the *Traverse City Record Eagle*, also in Michigan, W.E. Moranville of the *Des Moines Register*, Deb Pankey of the Chicago *Daily Herald*, Liz Reiter of the Louisville *Courier-Journal*, Ann Slegman of *Kansas City Magazine*, and Jody Wright of *Indianapolis Monthly*. One of the joys of writing this book was establishing friendships with these talented food writers.

At Emmis Books, Katie Parker and Howard Cohen worked tirelessly to get this book in the public eye, and Susan Young and Stephen Sullivan made the book good-looking and user-friendly. I am grateful for the help of my sister, Shelly Simonds, who generously dedicated her own journalistic skills to this book for fact-checking, as did Yvette Neirouz. Also, I'm grateful for the editing skills of Don Prues and Jen Lile, who erased my blunders and made this book more readable. My thanks to discerning friends and family who first suggested some of the great restaurants listed in *Best Food in Town*. My family was patient when I was traveling, and forgiving when I was physically home but mentally preoccupied. My husband Bryant and daughters Sophia and Lily were a constant encouragement and support. Thank you.

Table of Contents

INTRODUCTION

We all love comfort food. Whether we permit ourselves to indulge regularly or not, comfort food serves a place in our lives, culturally and physically. Researcher Mary F. Dallman of the Department of Physiology and Neuroscience at the University of California, San Francisco, studied the physiological effect of comfort food on our bodies and scientifically proved what we've known intuitively all along: comfort food makes us feel good.

Dallman's research, which appears in the Proceedings of the National Academy of Sciences (September 2003), found that food high in carbohydrates and fats curbs the release of stress-related hormones like adrenaline and the steroid cortisol. That means reaching for a piece of pie or a helping of macaroni and cheese when you're stressed may do more than just satisfy your hunger; it might lower your stress level, too.

Dallman and her colleagues are quick to point out that too much of a good thing is bad—comfort foods can make you overweight and unhealthy. That's why every indulgence should count. Don't just eat a slice of pie—eat a slice of the best pie. Don't reach for any barbecued rib, hamburger, or plate of pan-fried chicken. Eat the most fall-off-the-bone tender rib. The burger on the meltaway bun. The crispiest chicken, whose clear, peppery juices are forever memorable.

The best comfort food can be found in the Midwest. Restaurants from Kentucky to Wisconsin are full of fresh flavors and from-scratch cooking meant to be savored in a relaxed atmosphere, far from the stifling style of old-fashioned "haute cuisine." Patric Kuh chronicles a trend away from haute cuisine in his wonderful book *The Last Days of Haute Cuisine*, exploring the fine-dining industry's French roots and the stature and rigorous dining experiences associated with it. Those dining rooms still exist in the Midwest—Maisonette in Cincinnati and Les Nomades in Chicago are two of them. But ultimately the diner has evolved from accepting haughty food and style as the ultimate dining experience.

To me, the best dining experiences occur in a comfortable atmosphere, and that is a quality most of the restaurants in this book share. Exceptions may be urban hash houses or delis where surliness is part of the appeal. Nevertheless, dining experiences are one-time events. My positive experiences, and those of other restaurant critics in the Midwest, may not be duplicated by every diner. I only wish I had that kind of control! Restaurants are victim to human nature, but the restaurants included here are unlikely to disappoint.

Best Food in Town shares where to find the best comfort food and highlights a diverse range of restaurants. To some, comfort food may mean an open-faced roast beef sandwich with mashed potatoes and gravy. For me, comfort food is a platter of hot chicken flautas with creamy refried beans and light-as-air Mexican rice, or a big steaming bowl of Vietnamese chicken noodle soup (pho ga) with a table salad of lime wedges, bean sprouts, and cilantro, plus a bottle of hot chili sauce to stoke the heat. You may think of comfort food as a lovely tangle of fettuccine Alfredo sprinkled with parsley and fresh parmesan.

However you define comfort food, the Midwest is as diverse as all of these cravings and you'll find restaurants in *Best Food in Town* serving comfort food with diverse origins. All these restaurants share a dedication to food made from scratch and feature classic dishes within their specific food genre. To be sure, all food has some local agricultural origin, and not all the restaurants in this book serve food defined as Midwestern in a historical sense. But thanks to the modern age we can now get whatever ingredients needed to make any fare.

The local nature of cuisine has come full circle. Where locally owned and operated restaurants once used local garden crops in their kitchens, the practice was replaced by prepackaged, pre-prepped ingredients for the sake of convenience and cost (Eric Schlosser's *Fast Food Nation* does a great job chronicling this). And food made in this way can taste fine, but it's not glorious food. The best food is made from very fresh produce; the most exquisite food is made from produce whose strains are derived from the natural predisposition to be delicious (rather than hardy enough to withstand six hundred or six thousand miles of shipment), which is another way of saying fruits and vegetables grown from heirloom seeds.

Where can you find food with such an emphasis on flavor? You'll find it in small chef-owned bistros offering what I consider the upper-limit of comfort food. True, some of the menus escalate into fine-dining. Because of this I've included only a few chef-owned bistros in each state. There are many more—enough to fill an entire book—but that's a project left for another day.

Best Food in Town features some restaurants far off the beaten track; others are surprisingly right near the highway. All of the restaurants in *Best Food in Town* are a window into the culture of their geography. Chicago restaurants have an essence of their own. So do the restaurants of St. Louis, Louisville, and Cincinnati. But small town restaurants often have a personality that's most dear.

Early one morning I wandered into the Wilton Candy Kitchen in Wilton, Iowa, to find the first customer had already arrived. A gray-haired man stood stooped behind the counter pouring himself a cup of coffee as if he'd done it every day for the past thirty years. He stirred his white china cup with a spoon worn thin from years of use and told me the owner was in back making chocolate sauce for the day. If I wanted a cup of coffee it was behind the range, I could help myself or he'd get it. "Homemade chocolate sauce?" I asked. Having worked in a Baskin Robbins franchise as a teen, I know most chocolate sauce nowadays is squirted from a heavy plastic envelope. "Yep," he said, unsurprised.

What the customer didn't say, but what I understood after an hour with owner George Nopoulos (who came out front to make a grilled ham and cheese in an old sandwich press), is that not changing things is a matter of character and distinction. Cooking from scratch is more than a routine; it defines Wilton Candy Kitchen and hundreds of other restaurants like it. From-scratch comfort food restaurants can be superior in food and custom to places incapable of making a pie on their own, let alone something as easy to mass produce as chocolate sauce. Homemade chocolate sauce tastes better, but it also inspires an appreciation for community-based restaurants as a lost art.

As I chat with Nopoulos, he looks me straight in the eye and reads the emotions that run across my face. His questions are queries into who I am as a person; they are his attempt to know me, and I'm expected to be just as witty and engaging he is. Like Nopoulos and so many other restaurateurs in the Midwest, the restaurants in *Best Food in Town* are engaging. They are dedicated to serving great food, food that comforts us all in a uniquely nourishing way. I hope you enjoy visiting them.

How to Use This Book

Each chapter of *Best Food in Town* features approximately thirty restaurants serving some style of Midwest comfort food. Contact information includes the restaurant's address, zip code, phone number, hours of operation, and price range, plus a description of the style of the place and the food offered. If the restaurant accepts Visa and Mastercard, I've listed "MCC" for major credit cards in the description.

Since you may have Internet access while using this book on the road, I've included a restaurant's website when available. You can also use the address and zip code to get directions via an online service. I've noted which restaurants have a bar, and if the business only accepts cash. Please call restaurants before you go to them. Restaurants are small businesses at the whim of whomever is in charge—they might decide to stop taking credit cards, close early, close permanently, or—God forbid—stop baking coconut cream pie.

Of the thirty or so restaurants in each chapter, about ten of them are given full treatment, with a description of the interior, service, and food. These are the places I know best, but all of the restaurants in *Best Food in Town* are favorites of restaurant critics across the Midwest.

In addition to being an opinionated guidebook to the best comfort food in the Midwest, this book strives to be an in-depth dining source. You will not find another restaurant guidebook for the eight Midwestern states featured in *Best Food in Town* that lists as much contact information for as many restaurants. If you find that information has changed, please let me know by e-mailing me at bestfoodintown@emmis.com.

Again, please be sure to call ahead before going to any of the restaurants in this book. Restaurants go out of business with painful regularity, and while this book is up-to-the-minute regarding a restaurant's status, hours change, chefs quit, and restaurants shutter their doors. In a perfect world, before making any changes, a restaurant owner would think, "Oh, I'd better call that writer lady who was snooping around last summer and tell her we've stopped frying chicken." And then I could call and tell you. But don't you know, this world isn't perfect. Please call first.

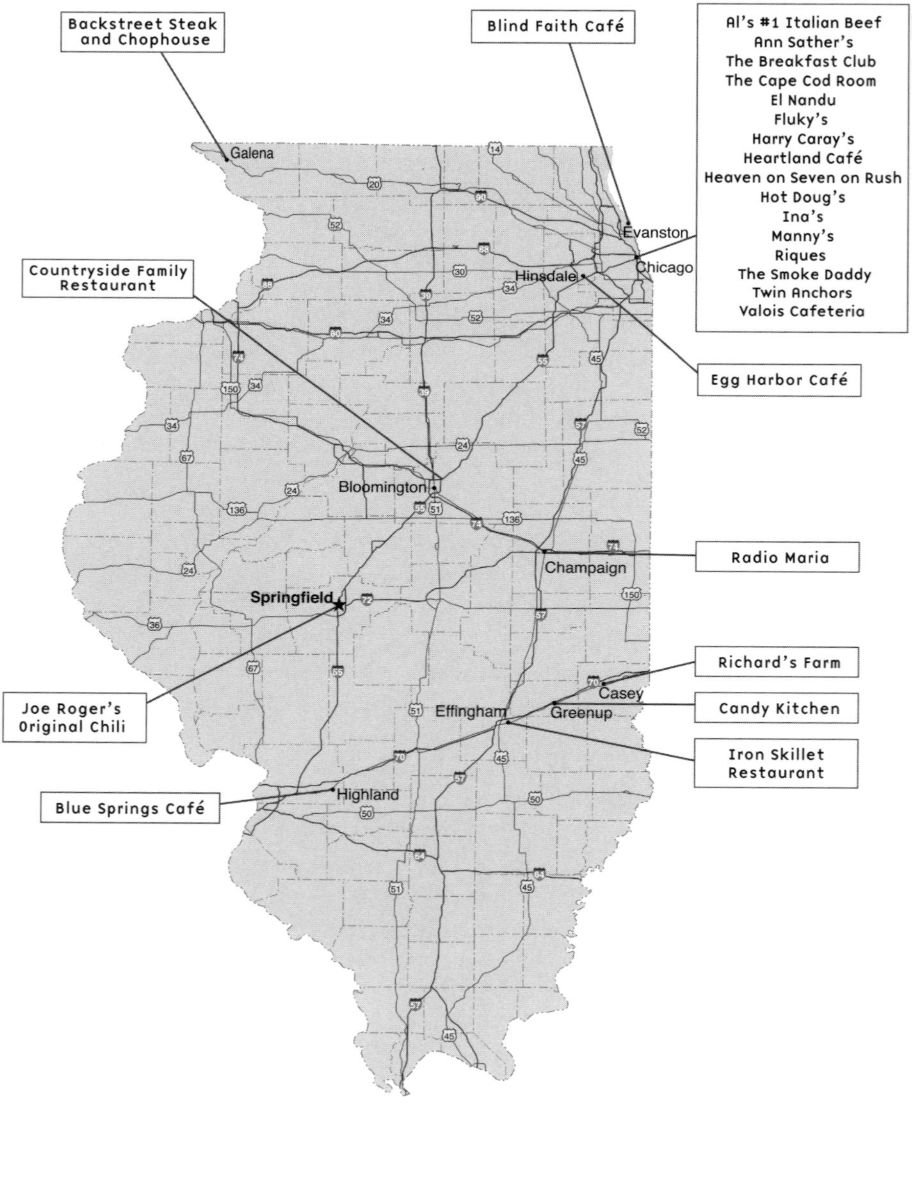
Backstreet Steak and Chophouse
Blind Faith Café
Al's #1 Italian Beef
Ann Sather's
The Breakfast Club
The Cape Cod Room
El Nandu
Fluky's
Harry Caray's
Heartland Café
Heaven on Seven on Rush
Hot Doug's
Ina's
Manny's
Riques
The Smoke Daddy
Twin Anchors
Valois Cafeteria
Countryside Family Restaurant
Egg Harbor Café
Radio Maria
Richard's Farm
Candy Kitchen
Iron Skillet Restaurant
Joe Roger's Original Chili
Blue Springs Café
Galena
Evanston
Chicago
Hinsdale
Bloomington
Champaign
Springfield
Casey
Greenup
Effingham
Highland

ILLINOIS

Hands down, Chicago has the best concentration of great restaurants—comfort food and otherwise—in Illinois. Don't let that stop you from exploring other parts of the state—and if you find good restaurants not listed here, please drop me an e-mail (bestfoodintown@emmis.com). But a culinary vacation to Chicago could keep you fat and happy for a week. One of my favorite restaurants in Chicago is Valois. This Hyde Park institution embodies everything that's great about a community restaurant: good, affordable food, a dedicated owner, and loyal customers who solve life's biggest dilemmas over the white Formica-topped tables.

Valois is great for breakfast—I had a memorable breakfast sandwich with ham cut off the bone here—and Chicago has plenty of suitable restaurants for the first meal of the day. Ina's and the Breakfast Club both find their glory in scrambling eggs. Further out from the city in Hinsdale, Egg Harbor's several locations offer a broad menu of healthy breakfast and lunch fare.

Regardless of what you eat for breakfast, thank heavens for lunch. Chicago citizens are lucky to have

Chicago red hots, the skinless all-beef hot dogs with plenty of snap ("snap" being that resistance to the bite which brings out our inner carnivore). This is not something to be taken for granted, especially the red hots at Hot Doug's, a small storefront with tables where Kendall culinary school graduate Doug Sohn serves a celestial version with hand-cut fries.

The greatest ethnic fare can be had in large cities because the population size can support the reproduction of regional cuisine. Rique's Regional Mexican Food in Rogers Park serves such regional Mexican fare as chicken in an almond sauce so creamy and savory it's mystic.

To the south, comfort food's king—the freshly baked pie—makes its appearance on the menu at Blue Springs Café. Here, the goal is two-fold: make a darn good pie, and make that pie as tall as you possibly can. These pies are tall and delicious, but don't forget to eat dinner first. If you're lucky, fresh walleye pike will be on the chalkboard menu.

Northwest

Backstreet Steak and Chophouse

216 S. Commerce St.
Galena, Illinois 61036-2216
815.777.4800
www.backstreetgalena.com

Dinner seven days a week beginning at 4:30pm

First courses $4–$10; Entrees $15–$40

MCC, Full bar, Reservations recommended

An upscale steakhouse on the border of Iowa on the Mississippi River, Backstreet Steak and Chophouse is a nice indulgence featuring prime, aged beef and prime rib on Friday and Saturday. This place doesn't break any new culinary ground, but alternatives like ahi tuna are on the menu.

If you want something more contemporary, with free-range and organic foods, try the Perry Street Brasserie, 815.777.3773, on the corner of Perry and Commerce streets in Galena.

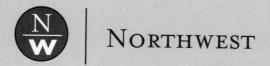

Northeast

Al's #1 Italian Beef

1079 W. Taylor St.
Chicago, Illinois 60607-4224
312.226.4017
www.alscatering.com

Monday–Saturday 9 am–1 am, Closed Sunday

Sandwiches $4.65–$6.50

Any fan of street food will sing the praises of Chicago Italian beef sandwiches without hesitation, especially those at Al's. But before experiencing the pleasures of this saucy, tender, garlicky sandwich, you should know one thing: Al's is a total dive. Consider yourself informed.

Walk in the double glass entry to a room with a bare concrete floor and a red, pock-marked counter. There, someone will take your money and hand you a sandwich: Italian beef, Italian beef double dipped, or a combo of sausage and beef. Take your sandwich and eat it in your car (provided your car is not a major financial investment—the sandwich is messy). People with nice cars smartly choose to eat their Italian beef on the sidewalk.

The sandwich is famous for a reason. Mild, tender, thinly sliced roast beef sits in a bath of au jus before a man with tongs scoops it up and piles it on a poppy seed sub roll. A mound of colorful hot peppers is pressed into the soft meat and bun and, if you like extra soggy food, the whole thing is "double dipped" back into another pan of au jus. A sandwich without this extra dunk is still dripping wet.

Ann Sather's

929 West Belmont
Chicago, Illinois 60657

773.348.2378
www.annsather.com

Breakfast, lunch, and dinner seven days a week 7 am–9 pm

Breakfast $3–$7; Sandwiches $5.75–$9; Entrees $8–$14

MCC

Multiple locations

Ann Sather's traditional Swedish food (roast duck, potato sausage) was recently augmented with trendier comfort foods like Asian-marinated short ribs and sweet potato gnocchi. The update was carried out by Carol Wang, a chef with chops from Trio in Evanston and Blackbird in Chicago, who has the sense to leave standards like the Swedish meatball sandwich as they are: perfect, on Swedish Limpa rye bread.

Blind Faith Café

525 Dempster St.
Evanston, Illinois 60201-4728
847.328.6875
www.blindfaithcafe.com

Breakfast, lunch, and dinner Monday–Thursday 9 am–9 pm, Friday and Saturday 9 am–10 pm, Sunday 8 am–9 pm

Breakfast $8–$9; Sandwiches $8–$9; First courses $6.50–$8; Entrees $9–$12.50

MCC, Wine and beer

Vegetarian

Blind Faith Café sits on a charming street near the shopping district of downtown Evanston, home of Northwestern University. The café is vegetarian and has that wholesome, idealistic college-town feel. But it's better run than your average college-town eatery. Owner David Lipschutz is a career restaurateur who's made the café a continual success over the past twenty years.

The sunny interior is broken up into three parts: a bakery with daily batches of natural, organic breads and pastries sweetened with honey and maple syrup; a small, casual self-serve café with a carry-out menu; and the restaurant dining room, with blond wood tables adorned with fresh flowers and colorful quilts hung on the walls.

Breakfast is served until three o' clock—Italian omelets stuffed with asparagus and mozzarella cheese, topped with chunky fresh marinara sauce and a side of brown, crunchy oven-roasted potatoes; banana almond pancakes; huevos rancheros; and fresh-squeezed orange and carrot juices.

The Breakfast Club

1381 West Hubbard St.
Chicago, Illinois 60622-6475

- 312.666.3166
- Breakfast and lunch Monday–Friday 6 am–3 pm, Saturday and Sunday 7 am–3 pm
- Breakfast $5–$10; Lunch $5.25–$8.25
- Cash

A server speeds past in a hot-pink t-shirt and a navy apron. Her fingers are stretched over four half-empty water glasses in one hand, and a coffee pot in the other. "You can sit over there," she motions with her elbow, "I just cleaned that one off." Tables are a hot commodity at the Breakfast Club from early morning until closing in the afternoon, because this place perfectly suits a roll-out-of-bed-and-waste-the-morning mood; it is ideal for the kind of day when the sun peeks out over the horizon and then suddenly it's two in the afternoon.

Located in a renovated old house in an up-and-coming city neighborhood, the Breakfast Club is filled with well-heeled professionals, families, and bedraggled twenty-somethings. A single room is scattered with bare tables and chairs. A small galley kitchen in the rear is a blur of movement, humming with the adrenaline rush of a line out the door every weekend morning.

The menu is simple: Pancakes (but corn pancakes, sweet and thick and punctuated with whole hot kernels), French toast (made of rich, eggy challah bread, stuffed with cream cheese and dusted with cinnamon), and enormous breakfast burritos partnered with homemade stewed tomatoes and onions that are spiked with chiles and topped with very sharp cheddar cheese. Simple, pure, perfect, essential. Breakfast.

The Cape Cod Room at the Drake Hotel

140 East Walton St.
Chicago, Illinois 60611-1545
312.787.2200
www.dining.thedrakehotel.com/capecod

Lunch and dinner seven days a week. Lunch Monday–Friday 11:30 am–2:30 pm; Dinner Monday–Friday 5:30 pm–11 pm; Saturday and Sunday 11:30 am–11 pm.

First courses $9–$18; Entrees $16–$42

MCC, Full bar

Reservations recommended, business casual

The Cape Cod Room offers a timeless restaurant portrait. The menu is filled with classic seafood recipes like lobster Thermidor and bouillabaisse, crab cakes, and if you ask, shrimp de Jonghe. This last dish is a Chicago specialty—you may find versions of it elsewhere, but only in Chicago do they know how to prepare the real thing: with superfine toasted bread crumbs, garlic, butter, and herbs. The individual-size chafing dish is doused with sherry before baking in the oven and arriving at the table sizzling hot.

Walk in this exclusive restaurant and you immediately have a sense of being in the inner circle—the lights are low, the wooden bar is polished to an amber glow. Copper pots and an antique bottle collection adorn the walls. Tables are draped in red and white tablecloths below a layer of thick white linen.

The restaurant opened in 1933 and, despite its somewhat casual Eastern seaboard décor, became a fine-dining staple in the city. Nation's Restaurant News inducted the Cape Cod Room into the restaurant hall of fame.

Egg Harbor Café

777 N. York Rd, Suite 22
Hinsdale, Illinois 60521
630.920.1344
www.eggharborcafe.com

Breakfast and lunch seven days a week
6:30 am–2 pm

Breakfast $4–$8; Lunch $3–$9.50

MCC

Ten other locations

This is a sunny local chain with specials like the "Meggsican", which is three eggs, chorizo sausage, and onions topped with jack and cheddar cheese, diced tomatoes, and sour cream; cinnamon roll French toast; and Swedish pancakes with lingonberries. Soups like cream of mushroom and broccoli with cheese rotate daily.

The Hinsdale location is a clean, busy cafe with a nice mix of healthy fare and the occasional high-cholesterol, greasy-spoon dish like a skillet of breakfast potatoes with bacon and eggs. A seasonal menu usually includes South Beach- and Atkins-diet friendly dishes, like the "South Beach Albacore"—albacore tuna salad with avocado, tomato, and cucumber served on a bed of romaine, garnished with celery, red cabbage, and diced red peppers and served with a low-fat lime vinaigrette.

El Nandu

2731 West Fullerton
Chicago, Illinois 60647-3015
773.278.0900

Lunch and dinner Monday–Wednesday noon–10:30 pm, Thursday–Saturday noon–2 am, Sunday 4:30 pm–10:30 pm

Empanadas $2.25; Entrees $10.50–$17; Desserts $3.50–$4.50

MCC, Full bar

With a touch of magic realism, a zest for nightlife, and good, authentic Argentine food, this restaurant near Logan Square is worth a detour. It's a small space—one room with a bank of tables next to a small bar and a dance floor—but it feels more cozy than cramped. Rotating exhibitions of paintings for sale seem inspired by surrealists like Eduardo Matta and others from Chile and Argentina, and musicians perform tango and bolero for dancing Friday and Saturday nights.

The small wine list consists of Argentine and Chilean wines with reasonable prices. Likewise, the menu is stocked with specialties of the region, like empanadas (fried pastries filled with meats, cheeses, and vegetables) and churrascos (thin steaks charbroiled quickly and served with fluffy yellow rice).

The criolla empanada is a light, thin dough puffed with steam around a herb-flecked filling of ground beef, raisins, and hard-boiled egg. The camarones empanada is a liquid-hot blonde filling of parmesan and stringy queso blanco (a white cheese similar to fresh mozzarella) plus tiny pink curls of shrimp. A few salads stud the menu; a unique Latin-style potato salad with fresh vegetables and no mayonnaise is best.

Fluky's

6821 North Western Ave.
Chicago, Illinois 60645-4708
312.274.3652
www.flukys.com

Breakfast, lunch, and dinner Monday–Thursday 6 am–10:30 pm, Friday and Saturday 6 am–11 pm, Sunday 6 am–10 pm

Hot dog $1.79

Cash

Multiple locations

In a city famous for all things beef, Fluky's is consistently voted the best hot dog in Chicago. It's a skinless red hot tucked in a poppy seed bun and loaded with mustard, onions, sport peppers, pickle relish, and tomato slices.

Harry Caray's

33 West Kinzie St.
Chicago, Illinois 60610
312.828.0966
www.harrycarays.com

Lunch Monday–Saturday 11:30 am–2:30 pm, Sunday noon–4 pm; Dinner Monday–Thursday 5 pm–10:30 pm, Friday and Saturday 5 pm–11 pm, Sunday 4 pm–10 pm

Lunch entrees $9–$33; Dinner entrees $11–$33

MCC, Full bar

Two other locations

Harry Caray's deserves a visit not because it has an authentic mom-and-pop flair. That's hardly the case—this is undoubtedly a slick local franchise, grossing $9 million annually in the downtown location alone, according to industry sources. But Harry Caray's has both shrimp de Jonghe and chicken Vesuvio on the menu, two Chicago dishes that have fallen off menus almost everywhere else.

Why does this matter? Because both shrimp de Jonghe and chicken Vesuvio are classic comfort foods. Shrimp that's steamy and succulent under a rich layer of sherry-soaked bread crumbs; chicken that's plump and moist with a crisp skin and salty greasiness, foiled by ruffles of bright green parsley.

Chicken Vesuvio is a legendary Chicago dish of chicken sautéed in garlic and white wine, with a dark crust of skin over fall-apart tender meat. Served with soft wedges of potato soaked in olive oil and garlic, Harry Caray's chicken Vesuvio has a sprinkle of peas on top.

Heartland Café

7000 N. Glenwood
Chicago, Illinois 60626-2803
☎ 773.465.8005
www.heartlandcafe.com

🕘 Breakfast, lunch, and dinner Monday–Thursday 7 am–10 pm, Friday 7 am–11 pm, Saturday 8 am–11 pm, Sunday 8 am–10 pm

$ Breakfast $3.25–$8; Sandwiches $4–$9.75; First courses $3–$8; Entrees $5–$9

★ MCC, Full bar

The Heartland Café is part of a larger community called the Heart of Rogers Park, including the café, a general store with natural foods and products, and a bar. Next door is the No Exit Cafe, a performance space made famous by acts like Steve Goodman and Suzy Boggus and by frequent Vietnam protests in the 1960s. The Red Line Tap, situated next to the Red Line El Train tracks on the other side of Heartland Café, is said to date back to the early 1900s. All of these line up next to each other and create a quaint, insular little world near Loyola University.

The Café itself has three sections: an indoor dining room, a broad screened-in porch, and an open air patio. All of the rooms sag a little bit from the Heartland's long history as a left-leaning social center since 1976, but convictions still drive the place and a certain earnestness shows everywhere, including the food.

The menu is enormous, with more than sixty breakfast items and eighty choices for lunch and dinner. It features the usual vegetarian suspects like tempeh, tofu, and brown rice, but this is not a vegetarian restaurant. Buffalo meat is stir-fried with soba noodles or in a char-broiled burger. Chicken is pounded thin and topped with pineapple in a tamari-maple glaze.

Heaven on Seven on Rush

600 N. Rush St., 2nd floor
Chicago, Illinois 60611
☎ 312.263.6443
www.heavenonseven.com

🕘 Lunch and dinner Sunday–Thursday 11 am–10 pm, Friday and Saturday 11 am–11 pm;

Brunch Saturday and Sunday 11 am–2 pm

Brunch $6–$11; Po' boys $8–$10; First courses $3.50–$8; Entrees $8–$12

MCC, Full bar

Three more locations—Wrigleyville, Naperville, and North Wabash

Heaven on Seven is a spice-lovin', butter-saucin', oyster-fryin' Cajun restaurant famous for its Wall of Fire (displaying some 1,600 bottles of hot sauce) and "big ass breakfast" with two eggs, chicken fried steak, and sausage gravy biscuits served at brunch on Saturday and Sunday mornings. At Heaven on Seven, Stevie Ray Vaughn's on the stereo and Mardi Gras beads adorn just about everything.

Heaven On Seven On Rush®
Carry Out Menu
Heaven on Seven Events
Parties From 20-200
Call 312-446-8969
600 North Rush Street • 2nd Floor
Phone 312-280-7774
www.Heavenon7.com
The Best Louisiana Cookin' Outside of New Orleans
Reservations Accepted • All Major Credit Cards

Louisiana classics, like deep brown gumbo studded with okra and etouffee, are always on the menu, but owners Jimmy and George Bannos aren't satisfied with mere imitations of southern foods. The duo has graced their menu with an original flair and made this place extremely popular (expect to wait for a table on weekends).

Sweet potato moss is a curious bundle of thinly shaved sweet potatoes twisted up, fried, and sprinkled with cinnamon sugar. It's a wonderful combination of flavors and textures, but don't expect to eat it gracefully. Sweet potatoes show up again in a risotto topped with andouille sausage and Creole sauce. Jumbo sautéed shrimp top a pile of savory parmesan cheese grits, and the dessert menu is chock full of pies: chocolate peanut butter pie, pecan pie, and Key lime ice box pie.

Hot Doug's

2314 W. Roscoe
Chicago, Illinois 60618-6211
773.348.0326
www.hotdougs.com

Lunch and dinner Monday–Saturday
10:30 am–4 pm

$1.50–$3

Cash

There are many reasons to love this hot dog stand with style: The theme song on the Web site (in a rock mix and techno mix!), the motto ("the finest in encased meats"), and the fact that owner Doug Sohn (a Kendall culinary school grad) sells a whole range of hand-crafted sausages like wild boar with roasted garlic, and jalapeño and cheddar pork sausage. Excellent traditional Chicago red hots and fresh hand-cut fries, too.

Ina's

1235 W. Randolph
Chicago, Illinois 60607-1517
312.226.8227
www.breakfastqueen.com

Breakfast, lunch, and dinner
Monday–Thursday 7 am–9 pm, Friday 7 am–10 pm, Saturday 8 am–10 pm, Sunday 8 am–2 pm. Closed Sunday for dinner.

Breakfast $3.75–$7.50; Lunch $3.75–$8.50; Dinner entrees $9–$15.75

MCC, Full bar

From the website address, you can see that Ina's is serious about the first meal of the day. Whole wheat oatmeal pancakes stuffed with fresh blueberries, homemade granola with dried cranberries, and a transcendant veggie hash are the essentials.

Manny's

1141 S. Jefferson St.
Chicago, Illinois 60607-4425
☎ 312.939.2855
www.mannysdeli.com

🕘 Breakfast and lunch Monday–Saturday 5 am–4 pm

$ $3.50–$11

★ MCC for delivery and carryout only

Manny's is a Jewish delicatessen serving a jaw-dropping number of entrees, sandwiches, soups, salads, and desserts. The most famous item on the menu is the corned beef sandwich—juicy, heavily seasoned meat stacked three-inches high with a slap of yellow mustard and cushioned in soft, crusty bread.

Riques Regional Mexican Food

5004 N. Sheridan
Chicago, Illinois 60640
☎ 773.728.6200

🕘 Lunch and dinner Monday–Friday 11 am–11 pm; Breakfast, lunch, and dinner Saturday 9 am–11 pm, Sunday 8 am–10 pm

$ Breakfast $2.25–$6.75; First courses $3–$5.75; Entrees $7–$12.75

★ MCC, BYOB

A small Rogers Park restaurant serving regional Mexican favorites like pollo en mole almendrado, a chicken breast simmered in a rich almond-mole sauce. Also tortilla soup and tinga, shredded chicken in a chipotle chile sauce.

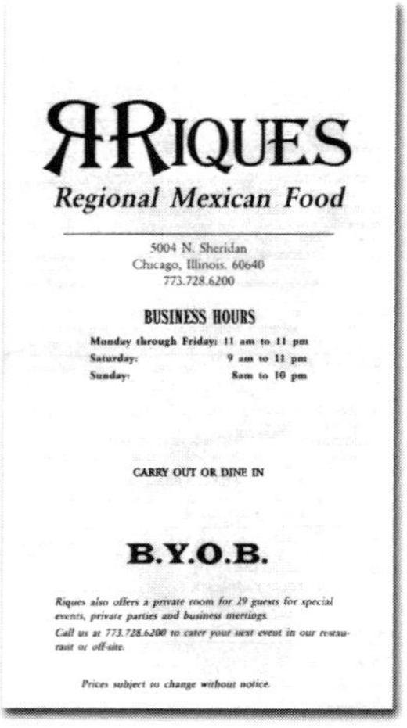
RRIQUES
Regional Mexican Food

5004 N. Sheridan
Chicago, Illinois. 60640
773.728.6200

BUSINESS HOURS

Monday through Friday: 11 am to 11 pm
Saturday: 9 am to 11 pm
Sunday: 8am to 10 pm

CARRY OUT OR DINE IN

B.Y.O.B.

Riques also offers a private room for 29 guests for special events, private parties and business meetings.

Call us at 773.728.6200 to cater your next event in our restaurant or off-site.

Prices subject to change without notice.

The Smoke Daddy

1804 W. Division St.
Chicago, Illinois 60622
☎ 773.772.6656
www.thesmokedaddy.com

Lunch and dinner Monday–Wednesday 11:30 am–midnight, Thursday–Sunday 11:30 am–1 am

$ Sandwiches $6–$7.50; Half-slab ribs $11.25; Whole-slab ribs $16.50

★ MCC, Full bar

Smoke Daddy is a no-frills barbecue restaurant and blues club in Wicker Park with a sink in the back of the dining room to wash your hands and face (instead of handing out little prepackaged nappies). Smoke Daddy smokes their meats in a smoker for several hours with hickory and fruit woods, and their ribs are the perfect precursor to booty shaking to live music in the narrow bar.

Twin Anchors

1655 North Sedgwick St.
Chicago, Illinois 60614-5745
☎ 312.266.1616
www.twinanchors.com

Lunch and dinner Saturday noon–midnight, Sunday noon–10:30 pm; Dinner Monday–Thursday 5 pm–11 pm, Friday 5 pm–midnight

$ Sandwiches $5.25–$8.75; Entrees $9–$23

★ MCC, Full bar

A locally famous barbecue joint with ribs, steak, chicken, and seafood, Twin Anchors has a darkly lit dining room and an old-fashioned feel. It's housed in a building built in 1881, and the restaurant's been going strong since 1932. Go early—there's usually a wait for a table.

Valois Cafeteria

1518 E. 53rd St.
Chicago, Illinois 60615-4503
773.667.0647

Breakfast, lunch, and dinner seven days a week 5:30 am–10 pm

$3–$10

Cash

Wait in line, order at the counter, and "see your food." That's the theme at this busy center of the Hyde Park neighborhood. Valois (that's Vuh-loy) is a Chicago institution. A student from nearby University of Chicago wrote a book about the place called *Slim's Table*, and Spike Lee reportedly wanted to use it as the subject of a film. But it's the food that makes Valois what it is: ham cut off the bone for exquisite breakfast sandwiches, T-bone steaks prepared to order, and prime rib with a baked potato for $9.

Southeast

Candy Kitchen

123 W. Cumberland St.
Greenup, Illinois 62428
217.923.3995
www.candykitchenonline.com

Lunch and dinner Monday–Saturday 10 am–9 pm, Sunday 1 pm–9 pm

Sandwiches $1.20–$3.50; Ice cream and sundaes $1.50–$4

The Candy Kitchen reopened in 2002 after the original owners closed it in 1960. New owners Wayne and Tina Swin bask in the old-fashioned glow of an American soda fountain, making ice creams, candies, and fudge in-house. Soups and sandwiches are also on the menu.

Iron Skillet Restaurant

I-70 and I-57 Interchange, Exit 159
Effingham, Illinois 62401
217.347.0447
www.petrotruckstops.com/food_option

24 hours, seven days a week

Breakfast $3.50–$8; Sandwiches $5–$7; Entrees $7–$13

MCC

The Iron Skillet is a truck-stop restaurant chain with three locations in Illinois (Monee and Rochelle are the other two). The restaurant lives up to the home-style cooking image it espouses: Breakfast, available twenty-four hours a day, is big on the sausage and gravy/ steak and eggs theme. Half-pound cheeseburgers and chicken fried steak punctuate the lunch and dinner menu, and everything's made fresh, darlin'.

Richard's Farm

607 NE 13th St.
Casey, Illinois 62420
217.932.5300

Lunch and dinner Sunday–Thursday 11 am–8:30 pm, Friday and Saturday 11 am–9:30 pm; Sunday buffet 10:30 am–2 pm

Sandwiches $5.70–$8; Soup, salad, and bread bar $8; Entrees $11–$20

MCC, Full bar

Richard's Farm sits in an old converted barn with a tall hayloft surrounded by faded wood wheelbarrows and wildflower gardens fluttering with butterflies. It's a lovely oasis, just off of I-70 across the state line from Indiana.

For lunch, a "hot bar" is set up with soup, salads, dessert, and a steam table featuring the lunch entrée of the day—pulled pork barbecue when I visited. Homemade salads sit in heavy crocks filled with finely ground, just-moist egg salad with pickle relish, ham salad made of salty country ham, plus homemade wheat and cinnamon swirl breads and a crock of homemade cinnamon-sugar butter. (An aesthete could just take a spoon to that crock and die happy. You can feel the sugar granules in the soft, light butter; it is such a blissful combination of textures, with just the right amount of cinnamon.) I really don't need to say this, but there's also homemade apple butter.

My attention strayed only by the arrival of a house specialty: Fried mushrooms. Now, ever since a multitude of haphazard fried vegetable platters in the 1980s, one does not wander into

the fried-mushroom terrain without trepidation. But this platter could inspire a whole new wave: The mushrooms are wiped clean (not soaked in water, so they aren't mushy) and dipped in a rather thick, savory batter. Then they're plunged into the deep fryer and brought to the table sizzling and golden brown. Not greasy, they're dry and accompanied by an absolutely inspired buttermilk horseradish dipping sauce.

RICHARDS FARM
RESTAURANT
Offering a pleasant and convenient place to meet with good friends, quality food, courteous country style service, and —most of all— value!
WELCOME
Gary & Diane Richards
607 NE Thirteenth Street ~ Casey, Illinois 62420
(217) 932-5300 ~ Fax (217) 932-4097 ~ richardsfr@rr1.net

Southwest

Blue Springs Café

3505 George St.
Highland, Illinois 62249
618.654.5788

Lunch and dinner seven days a week

Pie $4; Lunch plates $6; Dinner plates $9–$11

MCC, Wine and beer (dinner only)

Known for their "foot-hi" pies, Blue Springs Café consists of one big room with tables covered in blue-checked tablecloths. In booths on the far side of the room, road-weary travelers lean on their elbows, forking in fluffy bites of cream pie and draining bottomless coffee cups.

Chocolate, lemon, banana, and coconut cream pies topped with five inches of pearly meringue line the front bar. This is the Liberace of meringue, the Dolly Parton of meringue, the J-Lo's wedding of meringue. It is so tall it teeters but holds its shape through sheer culinary engineering. A forkful is light and airy and disappears in wisps of sweetness between your lips. But don't ignore the custard, which is rich and cold. The coconut pie was thick with white shreds of coconut, and the crust was flaky. Pie slices are $3.95, and perfect with a cup of coffee in the afternoon if you're road-weary.

A tall wooden bar at the entrance of the restaurant may lead you to think this is a good place for a cocktail, but the Blue Spring serves no hard alcohol. Wine and beer (of the mass-produced, small-bottle variety) is available at dinner, and dinner is comfort food unlimited: homemade pork sausage, pan-fried chicken, fried walleye pike, meatloaf. A blue-plate special at lunch of one of these entrees, or two corndogs (a fine alternative), is $5.95.

C | Central

Countryside Family Restaurant

Exit 120 off Interstate 74 near Bloomington
309.376.3302
Breakfast, lunch, and dinner seven days a week 6 am–8 pm
$2–$10
MCC

A community-owned restaurant, this favorite of locals serves solid Midwestern fare: Western omelets, home fries, hamburgers, and steak dinners.

Joe Roger's Original Chili (the Den)

820 S. Ninth St.
Springfield, Illinois 62703-1624
217.522.3722
Lunch Monday–Saturday 11 am–4 pm
$3–$8
Cash

Marianne Rogers took over her parents' restaurant, founded in 1945, and hasn't changed much. The menu is small and focused on chili—mild, medium, medium with a touch, and JR special. You can also try a loose-meats sandwich here, also known as a maid-rite: ground beef crumbled and steamed with an elusive mixture of spices.

Radio Maria

119 North Walnut St.
Champaign, Illinois 61820
217.398.7729
www.radio-maria.net

Lunch Tuesday–Friday 11 am–3 pm; Dinner Tuesday–Saturday 5 pm–10 pm; Brunch Sunday 11 am–3 pm

Brunch $5–$8; First courses $3.50–$7; Dinner entrees $11–$21

MCC, Full bar

This is a funky contemporary restaurant in downtown Champaign that combines Eastern and Latin influences with an eclectic American style. It's not far off of I-74 (about ten minutes, on Neal Ave.), and it's worth stopping for a meal, especially dinner.

High, tin decorative ceilings and exposed brick walls make up part of the artsy décor, and the menu includes trendy, contemporary food like pumpkin-seed crusted chicken breast stuffed with homemade chorizo and goat cheese, and tea-smoked salmon. There's a nice wine list by the glass. Radio Maria shares a short walking street with an art gallery, coffee shop, and bar whose café tables are filled with academics from nearby University of Illinois's Champaign-Urbana campus.

Title	Best Food In Town: The Restaurant Lover's Guide to Comfort Food in the Midwest
Condition	Good
Location	Walden Aisle D Bay 08 Item 6825
Description	May have some shelf-wear due to normal use.
Source	Prescanned
SKU	0KVOFY0022S1
ASIN	1578601460
Code	9781578601462
Employee	1dgordon
Date Added	6/18/2021 3:12:26 PM

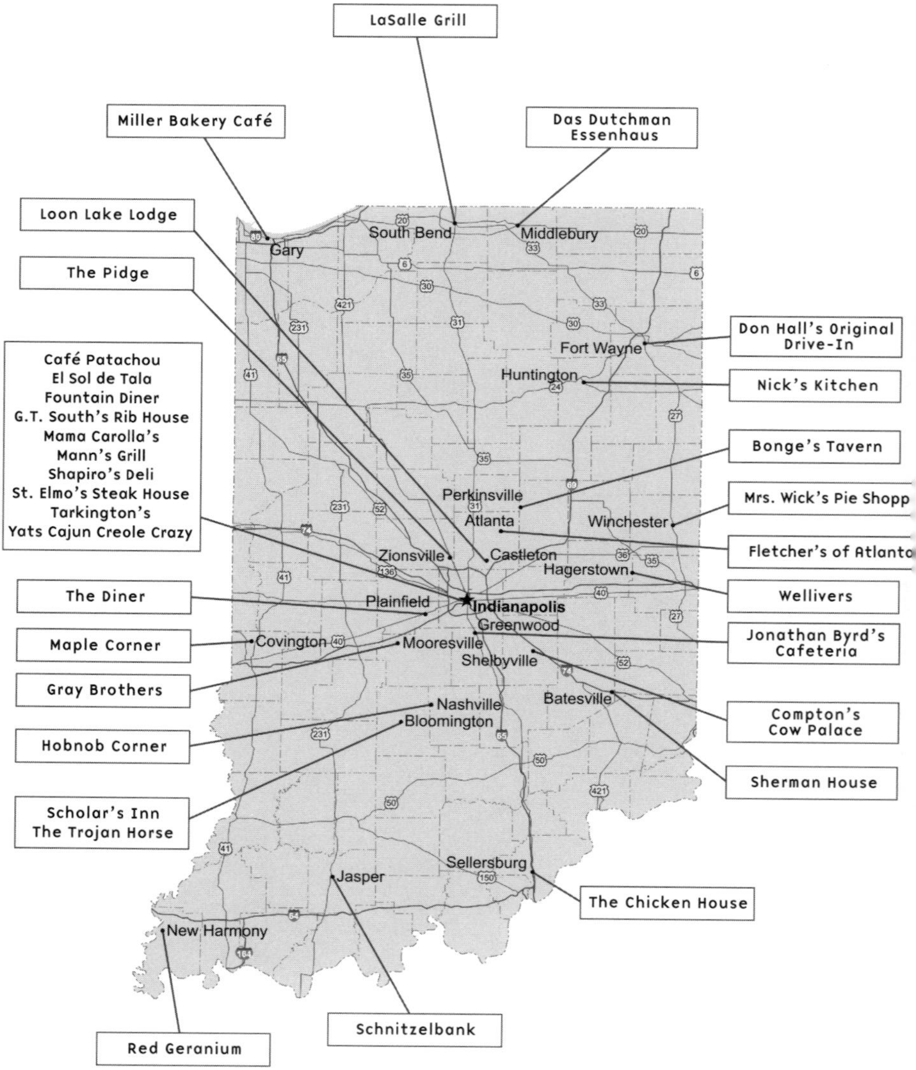

LaSalle Grill
Miller Bakery Café
Das Dutchman Essenhaus
Loon Lake Lodge
The Pidge
Café Patachou
El Sol de Tala
Fountain Diner
G.T. South's Rib House
Mama Carolla's
Mann's Grill
Shapiro's Deli
St. Elmo's Steak House
Tarkington's
Yats Cajun Creole Crazy
The Diner
Maple Corner
Gray Brothers
Hobnob Corner
Scholar's Inn
The Trojan Horse
Red Geranium
Schnitzelbank
The Chicken House
Sherman House
Compton's Cow Palace
Jonathan Byrd's Cafeteria
Wellivers
Fletcher's of Atlanta
Mrs. Wick's Pie Shopp
Bonge's Tavern
Nick's Kitchen
Don Hall's Original Drive-In
Gary
South Bend
Middlebury
Fort Wayne
Huntington
Perkinsville
Atlanta
Winchester
Zionsville
Castleton
Hagerstown
Plainfield
Indianapolis
Greenwood
Covington
Mooresville
Shelbyville
Batesville
Nashville
Bloomington
Sellersburg
Jasper
New Harmony

INDIANA

Indiana is full of ingenious restaurants, and Jody Wright, restaurant critic for *Indianapolis Monthly*, set out to tell me about all of them one day over lunch at Indianapolis's best Jewish deli/cafeteria, Shapiro's. Over plates full of chicken and noodles, corned beef sandwiches, and tapioca pudding, we discussed the unusual heritage that is Indiana dining. The state's cuisine is dominated by the cafeteria. "People in this state love cafeterias," Jody said. "The longer the buffet, the better."

At Shapiro's Deli in Indianapolis, owner Brian Shapiro dishes out kosher-style deli fare like fat, steamy corned beef sandwiches and chopped liver. On the other side of the city, Gray Brother's cafeteria serves its version of the cafeteria classic: Pork tenderloin sandwiches and crispy, tender fried chicken.

Indiana is also home to a number of quirky cafes. Bonge's Tavern in Perkinsville offers wild game and fiddle-head ferns alongside some of the state's best tenderloin sandwiches—the trick is in the parmesan cheese crust—

and chunky cream of tomato soup. Yats Cajun Creole Crazy in Indianapolis lets you have anything you want for lunch–as long as it's stew. Tarkington's (also in Indianapolis) takes the slow-food movement to heart, cooking everything from scratch and to order for an exemplary meal in a casual setting.

Fine-dining in the country is a recent Indiana phenomenon. Restaurants like The Pidge, Red Geranium, and Fletcher's of Atlanta take the best of suburbanity's outer limits—gorgeous country side, still night air, low rent, and charming character—and use them to delicious ends by creating simple, elegant bistro fare in a casual setting. In Northern Indiana, try LaSalle Grille (574.288.1155) and Tippecanoe Place (574.234.9077) for fine dining. Both are in South Bend.

NW | NORTHWEST

MILLER BAKERY CAFÉ

555 S. Lake St.
Miller Beach (Gary), Indiana 46403
219.938.2229

Lunch Tuesday–Friday 11 am–2 pm; Dinner Tuesday–Friday 5 pm–9 pm. Dinner only Saturday and Sunday 5 pm–9 pm. Closed Mondays.

$16–$25

MCC, Beer and wine

A small, sophisticated former bakery, Miller Bakery Café is owned by chef Gary Sanders. The menu combines international ingredients and techniques with the likes of Indiana pork chops and seasonal wild game.

Items on a constantly-changing menu may include a first course of just-crisp asparagus and smoked salmon with champagne vinaigrette, or braised short ribs of beef with wild mushrooms in a zinfandel reduction.

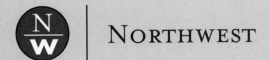

N | North

Das Dutchman Essenhaus

240 US 20
Middlebury, Indiana 46540
574.825.9471
www.essenhaus.com

Breakfast, lunch, and dinner
Monday–Saturday 6 am–9 pm. Closed Sunday.

$6–$15

MCC

Amish family-style meals, all-you-can-eat buffet, homemade sausage. Be forewarned: Amish restaurants are an industry in the Midwest. This ain't no hometown diner; it's a comfort-food megaplex.

LaSalle Grill

115 West Colfax Ave.
South Bend, Indiana 46601
574.288.1155
www.lasallegrill.com

Dinner Monday–Thursday 5 pm–10 pm, Friday and Saturday 5 pm–11 pm

$15–$34

MCC, Full bar

Fine dining, dry-aged steaks, seafood.

Northeast

Don Hall's Original Drive-In

1502 Bluffton Rd.
Ft. Wayne, Indiana 46809-1303
260.747.7509
www.donhalls.com

Breakfast, lunch, and dinner
Monday–Thursday 6 am–10 pm, Friday and Saturday 6 am–11 pm

$5–$10

MCC

Homemade onion rings, T-bone steaks, and BLTs. Next door is Don Hall's Food Factory Express—famous for ribs.

Nick's Kitchen

506 N. Jefferson St.
Huntington, Indiana 46750
260.356.6618

Breakfast, lunch, and dinner Monday–Friday 6 am–2 pm and 4 pm–8 pm; Breakfast and lunch Saturday 6 am–2 pm. Closed Sunday.

$5–$8

MCC

Apple dumplings, butterscotch pie, breaded tenderloin sandwiches.

E | East

Mrs. Wick's Pie Shoppe

100 North Cherry St.
Winchester, Indiana 47394
765.584.7437
restaurant@wickspies.com

Breakfast, lunch, and dinner Monday–Friday 6 am–7 pm; Breakfast and lunch Saturday 6 am–2 pm. Closed Sunday.

$5–$8

Cash

Sugar cream pie, savory pies, homemade soups.

Wellivers

State Road 38
Hagerstown, Indiana 47346
765.489.4131

Lunch Sunday 11 am–7pm; Dinner Thursday–Sunday 4:30 pm–8:30 pm

$14–$18

MCC, Full bar

One-hundred-item smorgasbord, roast beef, pan-fried chicken, chicken livers, and homemade bread.

SOUTHEAST

THE CHICKEN HOUSE

7180 Highway 111
Sellersburg, Indiana 47172-9240
812.246.9485

Lunch and dinner Monday–Saturday 11 am–8 pm

$5–$11

MCC, Beer and wine

Fried pork chops, fried chicken, homemade rolls, dumplings.

SHERMAN HOUSE

35 South Main St.
Batesville, Indiana
47006
812.934.1000

Breakfast, lunch, and dinner seven days a week 6:30 am–8:45 pm

$3–$30

MCC, Full bar

German food: potato pancakes and apple strudel with brandy sauce.

Sherman House
A Century and a Half
Old Restaurant and Inn
Established 1852
Southern Indiana's
Finest Cuisine.
A lodging &
dining favorite
of travelers
since 1852.

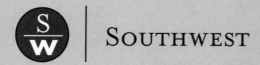

SW | Southwest

Red Geranium

504 North St.
New Harmony, Indiana 47631
812.682.4431
www.redg.com

Lunch and dinner Tuesday–Sunday 11 am–10 pm

Lunch $3–$9; Dinner first courses $2.50–$11; Dinner entrees $14–$30

MCC, Full bar

White tablecloth restaurant with lobster bisque, sautéed quail with shiitake mushrooms and port wine sauce, pacific escolar and chateaubriand for two, plus children's menu. Bed and breakfast next door.

Schnitzelbank

393 3rd Ave., Highway 162 S.
Jasper, Indiana 47546
812.482.2640
www.schnitzelbank.com

Lunch and dinner Monday–Saturday 10 am–9 pm. Closed Sunday.

$8–$40

MCC, Full bar

German food: schnitzel, potato glaze, sausages, salad bar.

West

Maple Corner

1126 Liberty St.
Covington, Indiana 47932
765.793.2224
www.maplecornerrestaurant.com

Dinner Tuesday–Saturday 4:30 pm–9 pm,
Sunday 11:30 am–8:30 pm

$10–$20

MCC, Full bar

Steaks cooked over woodburning fire; catfish.

C | Central

Bonge's Tavern

9830 W. 280 North
Perkinsville, Indiana 46011
765.734.1625
www.bongestavern.com

Dinner Tuesday–Thursday 4:30 pm–9 pm,
Friday and Saturday 4:30 pm–10 pm

Dinner entrees $17–$24

MCC, Full bar

Chef/owner Tony Huelster's restaurant is whimsical Midwest to the core. The tavern sits in a roadhouse that's been serving "beer and grub since 1847." When Huelster bought it in 1999, the entire place was gutted except for a mahogany bar with marble pillars. The renovated space is handsome but humble and heavy on the kitsch: a screened-in porch waiting area has creaky-cold old metal lawn chairs, and the bill arrives tucked under a mini box of Lemonheads candy.

On the wall, a chalkboard announces the menu: Seasonal items like wild game, applewood-smoked meats and sautéed chanterelle mushrooms and fiddlehead ferns. Bonge's Tavern still draws a local crowd who come more for the house specialty than the gourmet dishes. The Perkinsville Pork is a variation on Indiana's traditional pork tenderloin sandwich, pounded schnitzel-thin with a tantalizing, crispy parmesan cheese crust. Partnered with Huelster's chunky tomato soup, this food is cause for a detour. But be forewarned—there's often a wait for a table.

Café Patachou

4911 N. Pennsylvania St.
Indianapolis, Indiana 46205-1034
317.925.2823
www.cafepatachou.com

Breakfast and lunch Monday–Friday 7 am–3 pm, Saturday and Sunday 8 am–2 pm

$2.25–$9.25

MCC

Two more locations—8691 River Crossing Boulevard, Indianapolis, 317.815.0765; 4733 126th Street, Carmel, 317.569.0965

Café Patachou is always kind of busy. Just as you'd expect to wait for a table at ten on a Saturday morning, there may not be space for you at the long counter on Wednesday at eight a.m. Luckily there's always a stack of the day's newspapers on hand and for parents, a children's corner is stocked with toys, building blocks, and tyke-sized chairs. Café Patachou's breakfast and lunch menu is studded with homemade goodies like "house-made granola" with sun-dried Michigan cherries and almonds, homemade soups with organic vegetables, chemical-free meats, and good strong specialty coffee drinks.

Compton's Cow Palace

318 N. Harrison St.
Shelbyville, Indiana 46176-1312
317.392.4889

Lunch and dinner seven days a week until 9 pm

Lunch $3–$5; Dinner $6–$8

MCC ($5 minimum)

Compton's offers tenderloin sandwiches, hamburgers, and ice cream sundaes.

The Diner

3122 E. Main St.
Plainfield, Indiana 46168
317.839.9464
Breakfast, lunch, and dinner Monday–Saturday 5:30 am–9:30 pm, Sunday 8 am–2 pm
$5–$8
Cash

Breaded tenderloins, pattymelts, chili.

El Sol de Tala

2444 E. Washington St.
Indianapolis, Indiana 46201
317.635.8252
Lunch and dinner Monday–Saturday
First courses $2–$6; Entrees $9–$12
MCC, Full bar

This place could qualify as "best place to dine if you don't want to miss the soccer game." In a long, narrow bar, a Spanish-language station shows a crowded stadium and green soccer field dotted with red and white jerseys. Announcers give rapid-fire commentaries occasionally punctuated by a long, echoing "Goal!" At which time, everything in the place stops: the bartender stops mixing margaritas, the servers rush in from the dining room, and most of them trade high fives and smile, though a few shrug and groan.

Even if a soccer game on TV isn't your idea of a good time, the festivity of El Sol de Tala is addicting, and so is the food. Carne con chile y papas is a thin, fried steak atop fried potatoes and spicy homemade salsa. Tostada de seviche features fish cooked in a marinade of lemon juice, cilantro, onion, tomatoes, and serrano chile peppers. It's piled on a corn tostada and the crunchy and salty and tart and spicy dish is entirely memorable.

Fletcher's of Atlanta

185 W. Main St.
Atlanta, Indiana 46031-9762
765.292.2777

Dinner Tuesday–Saturday 5 pm–10 pm

First courses $5–$10; Entrees $16–$33

MCC, Full bar

Fletcher Boyd, chef/owner at Fletcher's of Atlanta, calls his menu "contemporary Hoosier eclectic." Contemporary Hoosier eclectic? What a funny guy! But really, contemporary hoosier eclectic is kind of a genre. There are quite a few little bistros around the state doing it, and none do it better than Fletcher's.

Like any contemporary bistro worth its sea salt, Fletcher's menu changes with the seasons and is built upon local products, like shagbark hickory syrup from Brown County. The menu ranges from wild morel mushrooms in the spring to venison in the winter, and recipe inspirations span the globe from Thai relish with free range chicken to Indiana pork loin and scalloped potatoes.

Fountain Diner

1103 Shelby St.
Indianapolis, Indiana 46203-1905
317.686.6019
www.fountainsquareindy.com

Breakfast, lunch, and dinner Monday–Saturday 8 am–9 pm, Sunday 10 am–5 pm

$2–$6

MCC, Full bar

Burgers, tenderloin sandwiches, soda fountain, and ice cream sundaes.

G.T. South's Rib House

5711 E. 71st St.
Indianapolis, Indiana 46220
317.849.6997

Lunch and dinner Monday–Saturday 10 am–10 pm. Closed Sunday.

$3–$18

MCC, Full bar

Pulled pork, BBQ ribs and chicken, smoked turkey breast.

Gray Brothers

555 S. Indiana 67
Mooresville, Indiana 46158-1713

317.831.3345

Lunch and dinner seven days a week 11 am–8:30 pm

$3.50–$8.50

MCC

A long line snakes along a winding series of roped partitions in the front hall of Gray Brothers Cafeteria in Mooresville. Indiana is famous for its cafeterias and there's steep competition in the field, including MCL's twenty-seven locations, Jonathan Byrd's longest buffet line and Laughner's cafeteria's carry-out empire.

But Gray Brothers tops my list, in part because there's only one of them and within the overwhelming heft that is all cafeterias, Gray Brothers seems the most manageable. The Gray family lives in Mooresville and concentrates on running a perfect ship—plating jello salads, ringing the register, and cleaning off tables. The current location has been in business since 1969 when the second generation took over. The first Gray Brothers was founded in 1944.

When family restaurants survive and thrive over time, it's usually because of a sincerity and earnestness you can't buy ...

but you sure can eat it! Fried chicken is the bestseller here. It's always fresh and sputtering from the fryer, thick-skinned and savory. Should you wish to partake in a different entree, there are a dozen more to choose from, plus salads, soups, sandwiches, veggies, desserts …

Hobnob Corner

17 West Main St.
Nashville, Indiana 47448
☎ 812.988.4114

🕘 Breakfast and lunch Monday–Tuesday 8 am–3 pm; Breakfast, lunch, and dinner Wednesday, Thursday, and Sunday 8 am–7:30 pm, Friday and Saturday 8 am–8:30 pm

$ $6–$11

★ MCC, Wine

Homemade soups, gourmet sandwiches, salad bar.

Jonathan Byrd's Cafeteria

100 Byrd Way
Greenwood, Indiana 46143-9724
☎ 317.881.8888
www.jonathanbyrds.com

🕘 Lunch and dinner seven days a week 11 am–8 pm

$ $8–$10

★ MCC

Claims to be the largest cafeteria in the world. Caramel bread pudding, roast turkey, pot pie, homemade soups.

Loon Lake Lodge

6880 E. 82nd St.
Castleton, Indiana 46250-1508
317.845.9011
www.loonlakelodge.com

Lunch and dinner Monday–Thursday 11 am–10 pm, Friday and Saturday 11 am–11 pm, Sunday 10 am–9 pm; Brunch Sunday 10 am–3 pm

$8–$28

MCC, Full bar

A suburban restaurant specializing in wild game like bison and elk, Loon Lake Lodge is part mountain-man fetish, part restaurant. It's located just outside of Indianapolis and not really as "far out" as it pretends—you'll find plenty of citified entrees like shrimp scampi, plus a children's menu.

Mama Carolla's

1031 E. 54th St.
Indianapolis, Indiana 46220-3219
317.259.9412

Dinner Tuesday–Saturday 5 pm–9:30 pm

First courses $4–$10; entrees $11–$19

MCC, Full bar

Tucked in a white stucco house in the funky neighborhood crossroads of Broad Ripple and Meridian-Kessler, Mama Carolla's is a family-owned neighborhood restaurant patterned after the old-fashioned Italian restaurants that popped up out West in the mid-1900s. A series of intimate dining rooms wind their way past wrought iron railings and arched porticos to a bar in the rear—an ideal spot to enjoy an old-fashioned or a Tom Collins cocktail with a plate of fried ravioli while waiting for a table in the dining room.

The menu is loaded with standard-bearers like veal Marsala, a plate of veal cutlets, mushrooms, and herbs sautéed in sweet Marsala wine; lemony chicken piccata, pounded thin and sautéed with capers and garlic; and succulent, buttery shrimp scampi topped with Italian parsley and served on a bed of angel hair pasta.

Mann's Grill

1214 S. Tibbs Ave.
Indianapolis, Indiana 46241-4128
317.241.5801

Breakfast and dinner Monday–Friday 5 am–9 pm. Closed Sundays

$6–$8

Cash

Baked ham, Swiss steak, turkey Manhattan, homemade pies.

The Pidge

60 S. Elm St.
Zionsville, Indiana 46077
317.733.1425
www.thepidge.com

Lunch Tuesday–Saturday 11 am–2 pm; Dinner Tuesday–Saturday 5 pm–9 pm

Lunch $7–$8; Dinner $11–$27

MCC, Full bar

Gourmet, seasonal dining featuring local ingredients. Chef Casey Lee Harmeson takes a contemporary approach to pork chops (paired with walnut and dried-cherry chutney) and sweet peppers stuffed with rye berries and goat cheese and topped with spinach pesto.

Scholar's Inn

717 N. College
Bloomington, Indiana 47404
812.332.1862
www.scholarsinn.com
scholarsinn@earthlink.com

Lunch Tuesday–Friday 11:30 am–2 pm; Dinner Tuesday–Sunday 5 pm–close; Brunch Sunday 10 am–2 pm

Lunch $5–$12; Dinner first courses $6–$11; Entrees $13–$29

MCC, Full bar

Antique lovers and Midwestern gourmets will find kindred spirits at the Scholar's Inn in Bloomington, Indiana. The menu at the Scholar's Inn Gourmet Café and Wine Bar changes seasonally. In the fall, expect to see wild mushroom pate with roasted pepper relish, shrimp sautéed in curried lime butter, and beef Wellington. Scholar's Inn also runs its own bakehouse and is known for its artisan breads.

Next door is a 115-year-old restored mansion, which is the "Inn" part of Scholar's Inn; guests receive gourmet breakfasts in its six king-size suites. Close to Indiana University and downtown Bloomington, the Inn is a favorite destination in the fall, when Indiana University hosts Big Ten football games against rivals like Ohio State, and the leaves begin to turn in the nearby Hoosier National Forest at the shores of Lake Monroe.

Shapiro's Deli

808 S. Meridian St.
Indianapolis, Indiana 46225-1335
317.631.4041
www.shapiros.com

Lunch and dinner seven days a week 6:45 am–8 pm

Breakfast $2–$9; Sandwiches $3.30–$8.25; Dinner $5.50–$11

MCC

It's true that in the Midwest, we sometimes think of a utilitarian Jewish deli as exotic. Tourists may come to Shapiro's downtown location from the nearby mall to gawk at the "kosher style" deli food: "Wow! Real matzo ball soup!" "So that's a potato knish!"

But once the gawking is over and the corned beef on rye is on the tray, along with a bowl of hot borscht, a side plate of chicken and noodles, and a cannoli, you are transformed from rookie to regular in a simple step. Shapiro's food is wonderful.

There are now two locations of Shapiro's Deli, and the second in the suburbs is newer and cozier. But the curmudgeons among us may prefer the traditional feel of the downtown location: a wide open space with lots of no-fuss tables and chairs with metal legs, it accommodates whomever walks through the door with brusque charm.

St. Elmo's Steak House

127 S. Illinois St.
Indianapolis, Indiana 46225-1079
317.635.0636
www.stelmos.com

Dinner Monday–Saturday 4 pm–10:30 pm, Sunday 4 pm–9 pm

$23–$50

MCC, Full bar

Traditional, formal steakhouse with aged beef and extra-spicy shrimp cocktail.

Tarkington's

153 S. Illinois St.
Indianapolis, Indiana
317.635.4635
www.tarkingtons.com

Breakfast and lunch seven days a week 9 am–5pm; Dinner Tuesday–Thursday until 9 pm, Friday and Saturday until 10 pm

$8–$35

MCC, Full bar

Owners Ed and Bianca Chambers believe in simply prepared, pure flavors inspired by French and Italian cuisine. Nothing is fast here, as everything is made to order with fresh, local, hormone- and chemical-free products. Gourmet sandwiches join flaky, buttery onion tarts for lunch. Price-fixed three-or-more course menu at dinner might feature fig-glazed duck breast, haricot vert in lemony vinaigrette, and white-chocolate French buttercream cake with fresh strawberries. A wine and cheese shop attached to the restaurant can help you stock up on provisions if you're on a road trip.

The Trojan Horse

100 E. Kirkwood Ave.
Bloomington, Indiana 47408-3330

☎ 812.332.1101

🕐 Lunch and dinner Monday–Thursday 11 am–11 pm, Friday and Saturday 11 am–midnight, Sunday 11:30 am–10 pm

$ $5–$15

★ MCC, Full bar

Walking into The Trojan Horse, you feel as if it simply doesn't matter how many years have passed since your twenties—when you could sit with friends for hours in a wooden booth, downing pitchers of beer and shooting the breeze at an alarmingly slow pace about shockingly trite things. Come in here, bring some buddies, and take ownership of a booth again.

This anchor restaurant in Indiana University's hometown square serves big gyros loaded with sour cream dressing that's studded with spicy onions and chunks of fresh tomato. Fries are hot, beer is cheap, and a game is on the TV.

Yats Cajun Creole Crazy

5363 North College Ave.
Indianapolis, Indiana 46220

☎ 317.253.8817
www.yatscajuncreole.com

- Lunch and dinner Monday–Thursday 11 am–9 pm, Friday and Saturday 11 am–10 pm, Sunday 11 am–7 pm
- Everything is $5
- Cash
- Three other locations—659 Massachusetts Ave., Indianapolis 46204, 317.686.6380; 1430 North Green St., Brownsburg 46112, 317.858.1312; 211 S. Grant St., Bloomington 47408, 812.339.3090

Louisiana comfort food all the way, Yats's menu is written on a chalkboard and everything's the same price: five bucks. The menu changes daily but always consists of two building blocks: stew on rice. Menu choices run along the lines of jambalaya, chicken Creole, red beans and sausage, and chili cheese etouffee with crawfish (which is very good).

The atmosphere is funky and casual. A long wood counter is littered with newspapers and regulars nursing mugs of coffee. The wildly painted dining room is small but cozy and pleasant, and the staff is friendly and hip.

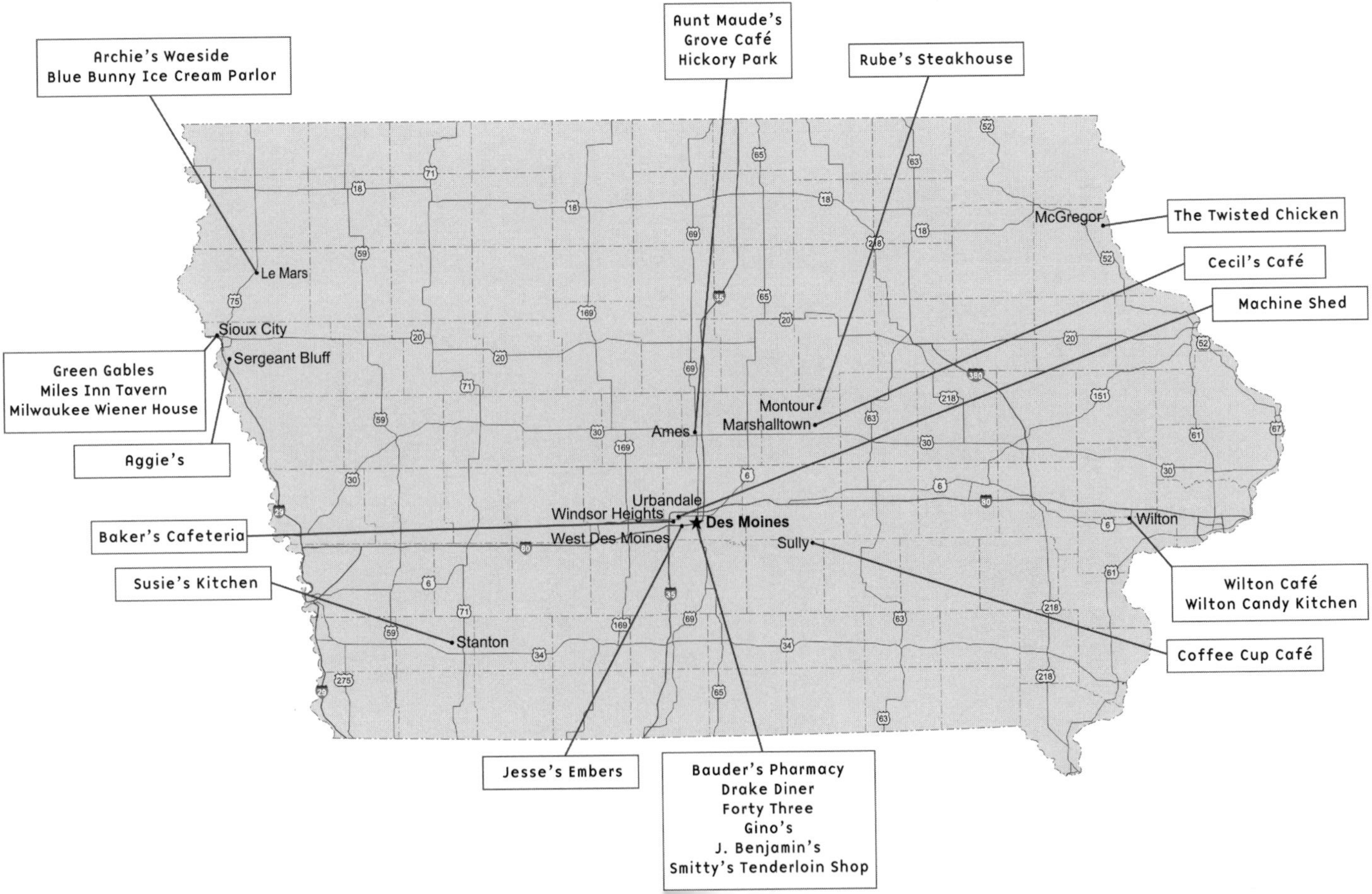
Archie's Waeside
Blue Bunny Ice Cream Parlor
Aunt Maude's
Grove Café
Hickory Park
Rube's Steakhouse
The Twisted Chicken
Cecil's Café
Machine Shed
Green Gables
Miles Inn Tavern
Milwaukee Wiener House
Aggie's
Baker's Cafeteria
Susie's Kitchen
Wilton Café
Wilton Candy Kitchen
Coffee Cup Café
Jesse's Embers
Bauder's Pharmacy
Drake Diner
Forty Three
Gino's
J. Benjamin's
Smitty's Tenderloin Shop
Le Mars
Sioux City
Sergeant Bluff
McGregor
Montour
Marshalltown
Ames
Urbandale
Windsor Heights
Des Moines
West Des Moines
Sully
Wilton
Stanton

IOWA

When you worry that the country has turned into a giant subdivision, that all the arable land has been devoured by developers intent on paving the horizon, drive across Iowa. The strip malls here are reassuringly far apart.

Likewise, while strip malls and fast food chains are what you see from Iowa's interstates, if you drive on smaller roads, into the towns and along city surface streets, you'll find the best of America: farmers' markets brimming with produce pulled from local co-op gardens, baby beets, yellow pear tomatoes, and small fingerling potatoes grown from heirloom seeds. Witness to this bounty are Iowa's restaurants, like Aunt Maude's in Ames, where the chefs have used locally grown, pesticide-free produce and poultry for two decades.

For an introduction to the state's cuisine, *Des Moines Register* restaurant critic W.E. Moranville met me at the Drake Diner near Drake University in Ames. "You have to order the rarebit burger," Moranville said. "It's an Iowa thing. Like a cheese burger, but with cheese sauce instead of a slice of cheese." The sauce is akin to Welsh rarebit—made of wonderfully sharp, aged cheddar cheese and beer. The whole thing was slippery and fat (with a half-pound burger), to be eaten with knife and fork, and sinfully decadent. Topped with onion straws, it could've lasted me all day.

After meeting Moranville, I spent days driving around the state and found what travelers looking for America already know: The way to get to know any place is to get off the highway, and if you do so you'll find people sincerely open to conversation. Time is amiably dedicated to momentary relationships in cafes and diners, where two clearly unacceptable commodities are platitudinous conversation and sub-par food.

Ice creams in Iowa are exceptional. Bauder's and Wilton Candy Kitchen have a long tradition of making them on the premises and serving them in polished, old-fashioned soda fountains. Blue Bunny ice cream, the maker of the original Bomb Pop, is also in Iowa and has an impressive ice cream museum complete with a video history.

NW | Northwest

Aggie's

2509 Canterbury Rd.
Sergeant Bluff, Iowa 51054
712.943.8888

Lunch Monday–Saturday 11 am–2 pm; Dinner Monday–Thursday 5 pm–9 pm, Friday and Saturday 4 pm–10 pm. Happy Hour 4 pm–6 pm. Closed Sunday.

First courses $4.75–$6.75; Entrees $6.75–$19

MCC, Full bar

Aggie's is a barbecue place with smoked chicken, ribs, sliced brisket, and pork shoulder. Hamburgers and steaks are also on the menu.

Archie's Waeside

224 4th Ave. NE
Le Mars, Iowa 51031
712.546.7011

Dinner Tuesday–Thursday 5:30 pm–9:15 pm, Friday 5 pm–10 pm, Saturday 4:30 pm–10 pm. Closed Sunday, Monday, and holidays.

First courses $3.75–$7.25; Entrees $11–$19

MCC, Full bar

Archie's Waeside is a traditional midwestern supper club with special care given to their twelve cuts of dry-aged beef. Archie's cuts the beef by hand in a chilled meat locker on the premises. The most famous item is not on the menu. The Benny Weiker, a center cut, twenty-one-day dry-aged filet mignon ($27.50), is available by special request. Entrees come with a nice relish tray, salad, and dinner rolls.

Blue Bunny Ice Cream Parlor

20 5th Ave. NW
Le Mars, Iowa 51031
712.546.4522
www.bluebunny.com

Monday–Thursday 9 am–10 pm, Friday and Saturday 9 am–10:30 pm, Sunday noon–10 pm

$1.99–$6

MCC

Visit www.lemarsiowa.com/visitors_guide/visitors_center

Blue Bunny Ice Cream Parlor sits next to the Le Mars visitor's center, whose claim to fame is "ice cream capital of the world" due to the massive output of Wells Dairy Farm, makers of Blue Bunny ice cream (and my childhood favorite, the Bomb Pop). At the visitor's center, you can watch a video on the history of ice cream before heading over to the old-fashioned parlor for fabulous frozen concoctions.

Green Gables

1800 Pierce St.
Sioux City, Iowa 51105
712.258.4246

Lunch and dinner Sunday–Thursday 11 am–10 pm, Friday and Saturday 11 am–11 pm

Lunch $5–$7; Dinner $8–$10

MCC, Wine and beer

The Green Gables was founded seventy-five years ago by Albert Seff, a Jewish restaurateur who brought corned beef and matzo ball soup to Sioux City diners. Today, granddaughter Jennifer Vollmer operates the restaurant with her husband, and while most Jewish dishes are gone from the menu, thankfully the rich matzo ball soup remains. Don't walk out without dessert—the Green Gables is serious about ice cream. The bestseller? Hot fudge sundaes with warm pitchers of hot fudge on the side.

Miles Inn Tavern

2622 Leech Ave.
Sioux City, Iowa 51106
712.276.9825

Lunch and dinner Monday–Saturday 10 am–1:30 am

Loosemeat sandwich $2

Cash, Full bar

Miles Inn is more a bar than a restaurant, but if you're in the mood for a burger and a beer, you really can't beat the loosemeat sandwiches here, called Charlie Boys. A loosemeat sandwich is ground beef, steamed in a spicy liquid and spooned onto a meltaway bun with cheese, pickle, onion, and a squirt of mustard. Wrapped in wax paper, it's the perfect accompaniment to ice cold draft beer.

Milwaukee Wiener House

309 Pearl St.
Sioux City, Iowa 51101
712.277.3449

Monday–Saturday 6 am–5 pm. Closed Sunday.

Coney islands and hamburgers $1.70

Cash

Milwaukee Wiener House may open at 6 am, but don't go there looking for eggs and bacon. It's all wieners all the time here, with a brace of coneys topped with diced onion and a bottle of Coke holding clout like manna from heaven. Add to it dill pickle, potato chips, or a bag of cheese balls, and you've got the perfect wake-up call.

Northeast

The Twisted Chicken

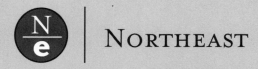

212 Main St.
McGregor, Iowa 52157
563.873.1515
www.thetwistedchicken.com

Lunch Tuesday–Sunday 11 am–2 pm; Dinner Tuesday–Thursday 5 pm–9 pm, Friday and Saturday 5 pm–10 pm. Closed Mondays.

Lunch $7–$9; Dinner first courses $5–$8; Entrees $15–$25

MCC, Full bar

Hours are reduced during the winter (the above hours are for spring, summer, and fall). Call ahead to make sure they're open.

Over the last decade, more and more classically trained chefs have moved to the country in search of a simpler but no less discerning life. The dream that a chef could produce menus highlighting the principles of California cuisine in Iowa is no longer a fantasy, as is witnessed by the creative-thinking entrepreneurs at The Twisted Chicken.

Cinematographers Neil Rettig and Kim Hayes fell in love with the rustic charm of Iowa and bought a farm, where they raised chickens with oddly deformed backs. They called the hens "twisted chickens." Years later, when the opportunity arose for a restaurant with the help of chef friend Tom Griffin, the fateful name Twisted Chicken rose to its righteous and full glory.

And the menu is glorious: For lunch, the daily menu might feature shrimp ceviche with kiwi and mango fruit or baked red peppers stuffed with orzo, fennel, and scarlet turnips. For dinner, entrees could be butternut squash gnocchi in tarragon sauce or roasted red snapper in prosciutto crust with strawberry butter.

Southeast

Wilton Café

12 W. 4th St.
Wilton, Iowa 52778
563.732.4115

Breakfast and lunch Monday–Saturday 5 am–2 pm, Sunday 7 am–2 pm

Breakfast $1.50–$5.75; Lunch $2.40–$6

Cash

When I am old and senile and forgetting everything else in my lifetime, I will still remember the hash browns and gravy at Wilton Café. Sliced thin, almost like chips, the potatoes are fried on the griddle until brown and flaky, then owner Robert Fterniatis slides them onto a plate and covers them with "gravy."

"Gravy." As if a name so insipid could express something so divine. I'll guess at the ingredients and say the sausage may have been browned in butter before cream from the neighbor's cow was added to the pan. It was so rich, with lots of crispy bits of sausage, a pinch of salt, and a hefty dash of black pepper.

This is a small, no-frills eatery, and it's very pleasant that way; the owners are on hand to refill coffee cups and welcome people in for breakfast and lunch. I'm told that Bob's potato soup is a big hit every Friday, and considering what he does with hash browns, I'm sad to have missed it on my visit.

Wilton Candy Kitchen

310 Cedar St.
Wilton, Iowa 52778
☎ 563.732.2278

🕐 Breakfast and lunch Monday–Saturday 7:30 am–5 pm, Sunday 7:30 am–noon and 2 pm–5 pm

$ Sundaes $2.95–$3.65; Sandwiches $1.95–$3; Phosphates and malts and shakes $.85–$4

★ Cash

Built in 1856 and listed on the National Register of Historic Places, hardly a doorknob in the Wilton Candy Kitchen is new. You wouldn't know it from the gleaming surfaces and polished old soda fountain, though. Owners George and Thelma Nopoulos maintain their ice cream parlor with the verve of die-hard historians.

The Nopoulos family has lived and worked in Wilton since George's father Gus opened the Candy Kitchen in 1910. George, who's worked in the shop since he was six years old, is small and thin despite daily indulgences in cherry cola phosphates and chocolate sundaes. He's an old-fashioned restaurateur who specializes in reading people just as well as he serves them. He stood across from me at his counter as I inhaled a scoop of butter brickle topped with wonderfully bitter chocolate sauce, and he prodded me with questions between bites. Before long I was showing him photos of my daughters and wandering through a kind of "Candy Kitchen" Museum / family photo gallery in the back room.

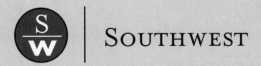

SW Southwest

Susie's Kitchen

404 Broad Ave.
Stanton, Iowa 51573
712.829.2947

Breakfast and lunch Monday–Friday 6 am–3 pm, Saturday 6 am–1:30 pm, Sunday breakfast 9 am–10:30 am, abbreviated menu 10:30 am–1:30 pm

Breakfast and lunch $2–$5

Cash

Stanton has a strong Swedish heritage made clear from the painted sign above Susie's Kitchen's door: Susie's Kok, a Swedish translation. Inside, breakfast favorites are Swedish pancakes with fresh lingonberries or a slice of one of the many homemade pies, the bestsellers being wildberry and fruit of the forest, with rhubarb, apple, strawberry, and raspberry.

C | Central

Aunt Maude's

547 Main St.
Ames, Iowa 50010-6008
515.233.4136

Lunch Monday–Friday 11 am–2 pm; Dinner Monday–Saturday 5 pm–10 pm, Sunday 5 pm–9 pm

First courses $2.95–$10.95; Entrees $9.95–$14.95

MCC, Full bar

An upscale restaurant with an avid following, Aunt Maude's uses as much locally grown and organic produce and free-range meats as it can get its skillful hands on. The setting here is elegant with linen tablecloths and oil paintings in gilded frames, but it's not too over the top for a nice night out on the road.

The menu changes a bit with the seasons but includes staples like seafood ravioli, Dungeness crab cakes, and smoked duck breast on a tangle of mixed greens to start. Entrees like local free-range roasted chicken come with not-just-knocked-off sides like sweet potato hash. Duck breast is partnered with andouille sausage stuffing and pinot noir sun-dried cherry demi glace.

Baker's Cafeteria

7400 Hickman Rd.
Windsor Heights, Iowa 50322
☎ 515.276.8432

🕘 Lunch Monday–Saturday 11 am–2 pm, Sunday 10:30 am–2 pm; Dinner Monday–Saturday 4:30 pm–7:30 pm

$ A la carte $2–$5, average check $8

★ Visa

This is a cafeteria in the dictionary definition: Grab a tray and peruse the jello salads. Looking for the best bets? Choose homemade yeast rolls and sweet bread, including blueberry muffins and sticky buns, plus midwestern favorites like ham loaf, baked macaroni and cheese, and pecan or raisin pie.

Bauder's Pharmacy

3802 Ingersoll Ave.
Des Moines, Iowa 50312-3413
☎ 515.255.1124

🕘 Breakfast, lunch, and dinner Monday–Friday 8:30 am–7 pm, Saturday 9 am–4 pm, Sunday 10 am–2 pm

$ Sandwiches $2.70–$4.25; Desserts $1.32–$3.00

★ Cash

The ice cream at Bauder's Pharmacy is famous. They've been written up in all the big food magazines—*Gourmet, Bon Appetit*—and were voted "best strawberry ice cream" by *People* magazine. Proprietor Mark Graziano was happy to show me the framed articles. He's proud, and why shouldn't he be? Graziano makes his claim to fame—lemon, fresh peach, and peppermint ice creams, to name humble few—in a little room that can't be much more than fifteen by twenty feet. It's jammed with freezers and little plastic tubs for the latest batch and stands as testament that the best food is created by hand in small amounts.

Bauder's ice cream is not overly sweet; it's dense, not airy, and a nice size scoop will set you back $1.51. Licking a rivulet of creamy lemon off the side of a sugar cone, I profoundly sensed the value of my dollar.

The soda fountain remains an integral part of Bauder's Pharmacy. Every single customer who walked in the store the afternoon I visited—even those who were picking up prescriptions—bought a dip of ice cream.

Cecil's Café

Highways 14 and 30
Marshalltown, Iowa 50158

☎ 641.753.9796

🕘 Breakfast, lunch, and dinner Monday–Friday 5:30 am–7:30 pm; Breakfast and lunch Saturday and Sunday 5:30 am–1:30 pm

$ $2–$6; Lunch and breakfast specials $4.25–$4.75

★ Cash

Painted bright pink and crowned by a gigantic cement rooster sporting a top hat, Cecil's calls out to you from the streets of Marshalltown: "Come, eat! The food is better than this exterior!" And it is, especially a breakfast of endless coffee and a cinnamon roll, or a fried pork tenderloin sandwich for lunch.

Coffee Cup Café

616 Fourth Ave.
Sully, Iowa 50251

☎ 641.594.3765

🕘 Breakfast and lunch Monday 6 am–1:30 pm; Breakfast, lunch, and dinner Tuesday–Thursday 6 am–8 pm, Friday 6 am–9 pm, Saturday 6 am–1:30 pm and 5 pm–9 pm. Closed Sunday.

$ $2.95–$12.95

★ Cash

The Coffee Cup Café is most famous for its pie, rhubarb being the top seller. New owners Robin and Darin Morvant intend to keep with tradition and offer seven different kinds of pie each day. Second only to the pie is another local favorite, the Dutch salad: iceberg lettuce with warm celery seed dressing topped with hard-boiled egg slices.

Drake Diner

1111 25th St.
Des Moines, Iowa 50311-4207
515.277.1111

Breakfast, lunch, and dinner
Monday–Thursday 7 am–11 pm, Friday and Saturday 7 am–midnight, Sunday 7 am–10 pm

Breakfast $3.99–$7.99; First course $2.99–6.99; Entrees $4–$14

MCC, Full bar

A retro-looking restaurant near Drake University in Des Moines, the Drake Diner has black and white tiles, big windows, and a shiny steel façade with hot pink and bright blue neon zipping across its name.

Sandwiches have a timeless feel in this casual place filled with a lunchtime crowd on a weekday afternoon. Tuna melts are piled high with chunky white tuna. Turkey sandwiches are carved from the bone. W.E. Moranville, my date for lunch, told me the Drake roasts its own turkeys daily and features the meat in one of the rotating blue plate specials (along with meatloaf and roast beef).

Rare is the day when a burger ordered medium arrives properly pink, but the Drake respects that request. My rarebit burger was a half-pound, open-faced, juicy burger with a Swiss-style sauce made of cheddar cheese (the real thing, not yellow cheese food) and beer. It was wonderfully sharp tasting, poured over the burger with plenty of extra for dipping in the tall pile of freshly made thin onion rings that scattered the top.

Forty Three

1000 Walnut
Des Moines, Iowa 50309
515.362.5224

Lunch Monday–Friday 11 am–2 pm; Dinner Monday–Thursday 5 pm–10 pm, Friday and Saturday 5 pm–11 pm, Sunday 5 pm–9 pm

First courses $5–$12; Entrees $17–$29

MCC, Full bar

Of all the restaurants in this book, Forty Three is one of the most upscale. I include it because restaurateurs Kristin and Jeremy Morrow use locally grown, high-caliber produce and meats in a seasonal menu. If you're out on the town and want to dine richly, this is your place.

Forty Three's menu applies international ingredients and techniques for creative takes on American cuisine. The ahi tuna appetizer called Tuna Poke is a salad of diced fish served with sesame crackers and wasabi. Barbecued pork spring rolls arrive with mango and corn salsa.

Entrees like soy-sake marinated sea bass with shrimp shiitake mushroom dumplings are entrée standard-bearers, though the type of fish rotates. You'll also find up-to-the-minute food trends like free-form ravioli in tomato-fennel broth next to comforting classics like organic beef partnered with baby fingerling potatoes and green bean salad.

Gino's

2809 6th Ave.
Des Moines, Iowa 50313
515.282.4029

Dinner Monday–Thursday 5 pm–10pm, Friday and Saturday 5 pm–11 pm. Closed Sunday.

Entrees $12–$20

MCC, Full bar

A classic Italian-American steakhouse in the heart of beef country, this place has one of the best versions of Steak de Burgo to be found according to my friend W.E. Moranville, restaurant critic for the *Des Moines Register*. Steak de Burgo here comes finished with fresh basil, butter, and plenty of garlic. Other hits are the fried chicken livers and a lasagna made of rigatoni, hard-cooked eggs, and meatballs.

Grove Café

124 Main St.
Ames, Iowa 50010
515.232.9784

Breakfast and lunch Monday–Friday 5 am–2 pm, Saturday 5 am–noon, Sunday 7 am–noon

Breakfast $1.90–$4.25; Lunch $1.50–$5

Cash

A pancake is not just a pancake at Grove Café. It is an ambition. As large as a dinner plate and an inch thick in the center, a short stack could be sliced like a pie and shared by a young family of four. If you've arrived at lunch and are in the mood for something salty, try the made-from-scratch cream of tomato soup. Whenever the daily special is meatloaf, regulars can't get enough. According to the counterhelp, "We always run out."

Hickory Park

1404 S. Duff St.
Ames, Iowa 50010
515.232.8940
www.hickorypark-bbq.com

Lunch and dinner Sunday–Thursday 10:30 am–9 pm, Friday and Saturday 10:30 am–10 pm

Entrees $3.60–$16.50

MCC

I looked over the menu at Hickory Park with dismay. It wasn't that the menu didn't look good—I was impressed with everything from the moment I'd arrived. Hickory Park has a convenient location, a nice building, good service, and a broad menu. But I was on my fifth meal of the day and I still had two more to go.

"What's the smallest portion of ribs you have?" I asked my sweet, young waiter. Assuming I was a small eater (a fine but totally false assumption) he helped me scour the menu. Every rib dish was a platter with two sides. I felt like the guy from *I'm Gonna Get You Sucka* when I asked hopefully, "Can I get just one rib?"

The answer was no—though he was nice about it—and I'm glad I tried the barbecue beans. Hickory Park makes sides from scratch using fresh ingredients, and the baked beans are smoked and slow-simmered with chunks of salt pork. My smoky short loin pork ribs were fall-off-the-bone, not too wet, and with the sauce on the side.

J. Benjamin's

5800 Franklin Ave.
Des Moines, Iowa 50322-6132
515.255.3725
www.jbenbbq.com

Dinner Tuesday–Thursday 5 pm–9 pm, Friday and Saturday 5 pm–10 pm. Closed Sunday and Monday.

First courses $3–$9; Entrees $7–$21

MCC, Full bar

An upscale-casual restaurant with a broad-ranging menu, J. Benjamin's offers steaks, pizzas, and ribs with upscale touches like a gremolata of fresh garlic and herbs topping its Steak de Burgo. Daily offerings of homemade soups and veal piccata make the gourmet happy, though it's comfortable for family night dinner, too.

Jesse's Embers

3301 Ingersoll
West Des Moines, Iowa 50312
www.jessesembers.com

515.255.6011

Lunch Monday–Friday 11 am–2 pm; Dinner Monday–Thursday 5 pm–10 pm, Friday and Saturday 5 pm–11 pm. Closed Sunday.

First courses $3.95–$6.95; Entrees $10.00–$36.95

MCC, Full bar

Second location—50th and E.P True Parkway, West Des Moines, 515.225.9711

Has Jesse's Embers' interior ever been exposed to daylight? This is a question one might ponder upon stumbling onto the dark red carpet in this dark red dining room. If you were alive and dining out during the seventies, you've been to a place like this—red leather banquettes, dark wooden tables with half-circle wooden chairs, martinis for the gentleman, French Colombard for the lady, and a Shirley Temple for the kids. But what separates Jessie's Embers from the steakhouses of your past is the aged prime beef from a small meat cutter in Iowa, and at Jesse's Embers' second location, a little special dish called Steak de Burgo.

Now, listen, I'm not talking about burgoo, as in the Kentucky stew featuring whatever wild animal runs past. Steak de Burgo is a center-cut, eight-ounce filet drenched in butter, garlic, and white wine, finished with cream and fresh basil. Got it? Go get it!

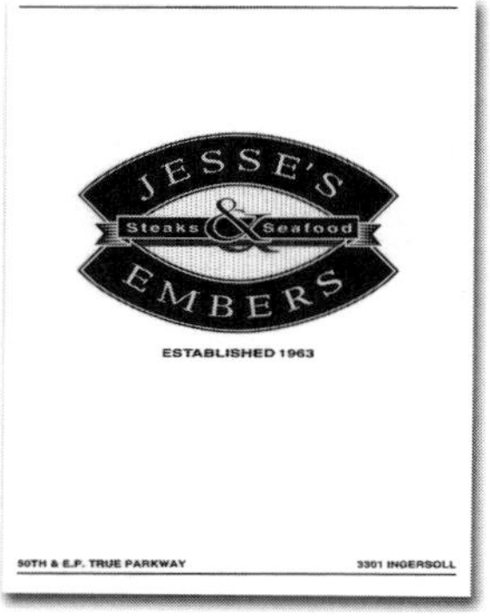

Of course, there are other reasons to visit this museum to the cocktail hour. Salads feature butter-soaked homemade croutons, soft and crumbly and seemingly made of yesterday's dinner rolls. Slightly oily, entirely addictive, and surpassed only by cottage fries, which are thin slices of baked potato, briefly dunked in the fryer and served spitting hot.

Servers wear starched white shirts and black aprons, and they have the ability to wait on six tables at once with absolute ease. The walls are wood paneled, and brass chandeliers cast low sparkling light across the intimate, if somewhat smoky, dining room.

Machine Shed

11151 Hickman Rd.
Urbandale, Iowa 50322
www.machineshed.com

515.270.6818

Breakfast, lunch, and dinner Monday–Saturday 6 am–10 pm, Sunday 7 am–9 pm; Breakfast buffet Saturday and Sunday 7 am–1 pm

First courses $3.99–$9.99; Breakfast $3.99–$8.99; Entrees $7.99–$21.99

MCC, Full bar

Multiple locations

Machine Shed's menu is about as corporate country as I've seen, with phrases like "fetch you more fixin's" and words "genuine" and "down-home" next to trademark ™'s. But forgive the countryfried hyperbole. This is a fine, family-friendly place to have a meal if you're in the mood for comfort food.

Out front, the Machine Shed is adorned with rusted John Deere tractors and bushels of corn. An employee sits husking ears over a metal bin (but on the day I was there, this was more of a prop than a preparation for dinner). A gift shop in the entryway is filled with miniature toy tractors, pink rubber pigs, and other kitsch that keep kids occupied while adults order drinks from the full bar.

Machine Shed's menu offers breakfast, lunch, and dinner, and "big" is the operative word for all three, with cinnamon rolls "bigger than a breadbox" and sixteen-ounce T-bone steaks. I tried a hot, flaky chicken pot pie loaded with chunks of chicken, carrots, celery, and potato. It came with thick sliced homemade bread and sides of coleslaw and the best cottage cheese I've ever tasted—milky sweet and icebox cold. The server said they get it from local farmers, and it's just not the same as what you get in the store. Amen to that.

Rube's Steakhouse

118 Elm St.
Montour, Iowa 50173
515.492.6222
www.dmdining.com

Dinner Sunday 4:30 pm–9 pm, Monday–Thursday 5 pm–9 pm, Friday and Saturday 5 pm–10 pm

Entrees $9–$36 (for a 54-ounce sirloin)

MCC, Full bar

Some people who really like meat feel it's entirely appropriate to drive across several states to eat a steak at Rube's. That's because the steaks are dry-aged and hand-cut and have an elusive character that makes you think the cows are fed a special diet of arugula salad and French burgundy. While I can't answer the question of the pampered cows, I am happy to tell you that, once you've eaten at Rube's and are pondering selling the condo in Miami for a farmhouse in Montour: Rube's steaks are now available for ordering online. But go to this little steakhouse first for the experience. In addition to steaks, you'll find an unlimited soup and salad bar included with the entrée price.

Smitty's Tenderloin Shop

1401 Army Post Rd.
Des Moines, Iowa 50315
515.287.4742

Lunch and dinner Tuesday–Saturday 10 am–9 pm. Closed Sunday and Monday.

Small tenderloin $3.10, large tenderloin $4.70; Onion rings single order $1.80, box $5.95

Cash

Smitty's has a lot of competition—pounded tenderloin sandwiches are a topic of debate in Iowa, and many places claim to be the best. But I like Smitty's. They bread their tenderloins by hand every day and fry them in boiling hot soybean oil. Likewise, the onion rings are made daily from scratch. Third-generation owner Benjamin Smith describes the king tenderloin for the uninitiated, "Well, it's like a hubcap really, and you nibble around the edges. It's good."

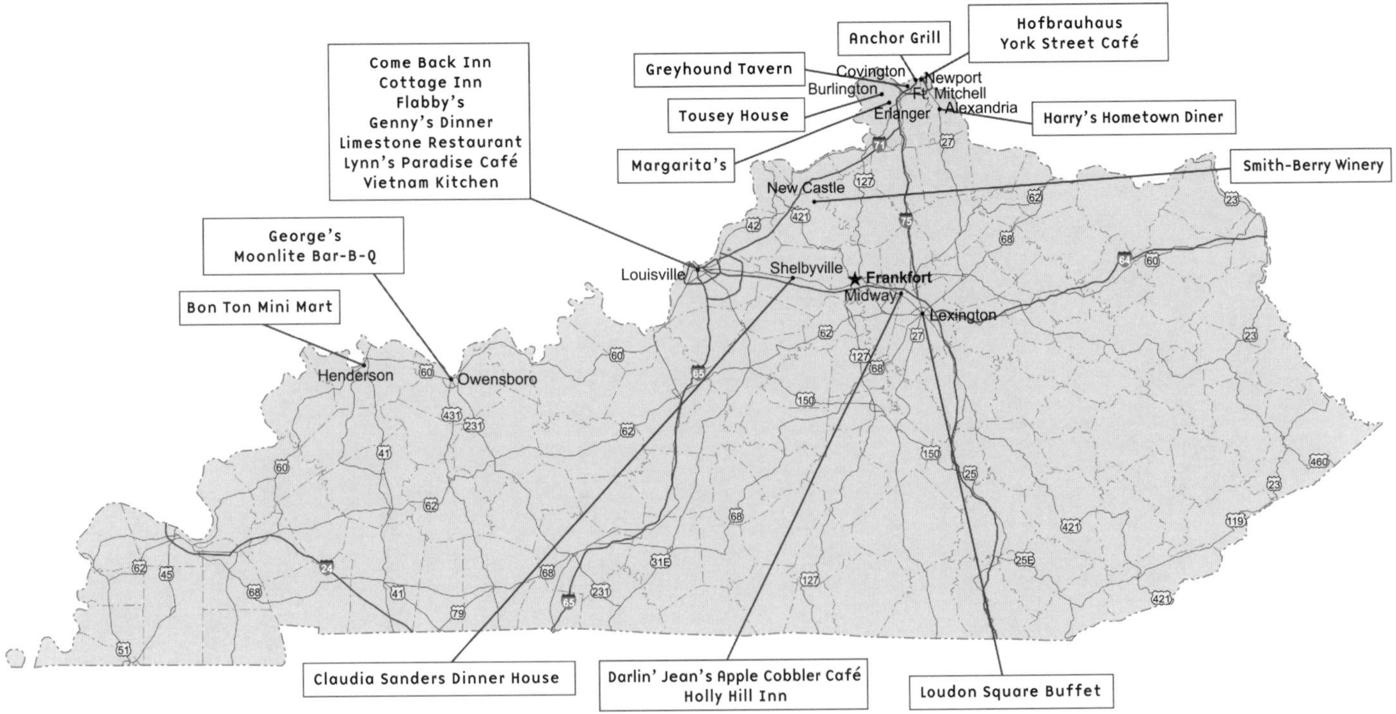

Come Back Inn
Cottage Inn
Flabby's
Genny's Dinner
Limestone Restaurant
Lynn's Paradise Café
Vietnam Kitchen
Greyhound Tavern
Anchor Grill
Hofbrauhaus
York Street Café
Tousey House
Harry's Hometown Diner
Margarita's
Smith-Berry Winery
George's
Moonlite Bar-B-Q
Bon Ton Mini Mart
Claudia Sanders Dinner House
Darlin' Jean's Apple Cobbler Café
Holly Hill Inn
Loudon Square Buffet
Covington
Newport
Burlington
Ft. Mitchell
Erlanger
Alexandria
New Castle
Louisville
Shelbyville
Frankfort
Midway
Lexington
Henderson
Owensboro

KENTUCKY

When I moved to Lexington from Cincinnati in 1996, the journey took a grand total of one and a half hours on Interstate 75. I didn't think life would be much different in Lexington, and it wasn't, except for the fact that people started calling me "Yankee."

Therein lies the biggest difference between Kentucky and Ohio. Kentucky is south of the Ohio River and sympathized with the confederacy, but its long borders with Ohio and Indiana do just as much to define its cuisine. Just like Ohio is halfway East and Missouri is halfway West, Kentucky has a foot in both camps. The downside of the term "Midwest" may be that a broad group of states are lumped together; the upside is the diversity of the states makes the Midwest unpredictable and compelling. Certainly that's the case with Kentucky, where the history of hunting wild game and stoking illegal stills has made for a profoundly unique and comforting cuisine.

The most exciting trend in Kentucky cuisine is the steady move to seasonal menus inspired by local ingredients like bourbon, country ham, catfish, and sorghum. The

Holly Hill Inn in Midway, Kentucky, exemplifies the trend, creating environs both cosmopolitan and charming. Ceramic chargers sit on white linen tablecloths surrounded by fine tasting glasses to complement the thoughtful wine list. The menu includes the likes of buckwheat pancakes with crème fraiche, caviar, and country ham.

Some notable restaurateurs in Kentucky rely heavily on local purveyors. When I asked Tousey House chef-owner Kristy Schalck, in Burlington, how I could contact her produce purveyor, "the Boys of Rabbit Hash," she paused quizzically, and then said, "Well, I don't know, they're really just a couple of boys from Rabbit Hash, Kentucky." They happen to be boys savvy enough to pick wild watercress and deliver it to Schalck's door before dinner. In Louisville, Jim Gerhardt and Michael Cunha poach fish in apple cider from nearby Woodford County and pair it with a barley risotto.

Of course, not all restaurants in Kentucky are redefining comfort food. Many are content with exemplifying the genre. Loudon Square and Claudia Sander's Dinner House are known for their family-style dinners and endless buffets, and Moonlite BBQ in Owensboro serves barbecue mutton and the state's great survival stew—burgoo. In Northern Kentucky, Covington and Newport are re-establishing a regional draw as a nightlife destination across the river from Cincinnati, thanks to glitzy restaurateurs like steak-house king Jeff Ruby. But not all top restaurants sparkle. Some simply charm. La Mexicana (859.491.3300) in Newport offers fare that runs from the pedestrian (goat-meat tacos) to the gourmet (seasonal cuitlacoche quesadillas), served with care by owners Ray and Susy Garcia.

NW | Northwest

Claudia Sanders Dinner House

3202 Shelbyville Rd.
Shelbyville, Kentucky 40065-9150
502.633.5600

Lunch and dinner Tuesday–Sunday 11 am–9 pm

$8–$18

MCC, Full bar except on Sunday

Family-style dinners with roasted meats, vegetables, and dinner rolls, plus an elaborate buffet on Sunday until 4 pm.

Come Back Inn

909 Swan St.
Louisville, Kentucky 40204-1809
502.627.1777

Lunch Monday–Friday 11 am–2 pm; Dinner Tuesday–Friday 2 pm–10 pm, Saturday noon–10 pm, Sunday 1 pm–10 pm

$5–$10

MCC, Full bar

Casual, family-style Italian dining specializing in Chicago-style Italian roast beef sandwiches with rich, spicy beef broth and melted provolone cheese.

Cottage Inn

570 Eastern Parkway
Louisville, Kentucky 40217-1854
502.637.4325

Lunch and dinner Monday–Saturday 10:45 am–8:30 pm

Soups, salads, and appetizers $3–$6; Lunch and dinner specials $6; Dinner entrees $7–$9

MCC

The Cottage Inn is a comfort-foods greatest hits restaurant. If you're craving it and it's a combination of starch and fat, it's probably on the menu here. Country-fried steak with country gravy, really good fried okra, and fried chicken made to order, plus pound cake, chess pie, and coconut cream pie.

Flabby's

1101 Lydia St.
Louisville, Kentucky 40217
502.637.9136
www.mazzonis.com/Flabbys.html

Lunch and dinner Monday–Saturday 11 am–9 pm. Sunday 3 pm–9 pm September–April (for football season)

Lunch $4.50–$7.95; First courses $2.50–$6.50; Entrees up to $11

Cash, Beer on tap

German fare at a traditional bar pub in a blue collar neighborhood. Order your "rolled oysters" (rolled in crackercrumbs and fried), pork schnitzel sandwich, or fried chicken livers at the counter and await a plastic basket of attentively prepared, cholesterol crazy, delectably fried food.

Genny's Dinner

2223 Frankfort Ave.
Louisville, Kentucky 40206-2407
502.893.0923

Breakfast, lunch, and dinner Monday–Saturday 8:30 am–10:30 pm

$4–$16

Cash, Full bar

Frickled pickles (that's deep-fried dill pickle chips to you), Sweet Daddy platter (one-and-a-quarter-pound hamburger with fries), grilled cheese.

Limestone Restaurant

10001 Forest Green Blvd.
Louisville, Kentucky 40223-5119
502.426.7477
www.limestonerestaurant.net
limestonerest@bellsouth.net

Dinner Monday–Saturday 5 pm–10 pm

First courses $4.50–$15; Entrees $12–$25; Desserts $4.50–$7

MCC, Full bar

Excellent wine list, five-course tasting menu $50, $75 with wine pairings. Reservations recommended.

Located in a strip mall near glass-tower office buildings, you might not expect home cooking at Limestone Restaurant . . . but you'd be wrong. Grits, fried green tomatoes, rainbow trout, and red eye gravy are all on the menu here. The catch is that these ingredients inspire creative and exceptional cooking. Grits are a neatly made white bed for succulent shrimp; trout is accompanied by a vodka-infused apple salad and a dollop of local spoonfish caviar. It's modern but comforting at the same time.

Limestone chef-owners Jim Gerhardt and Michael Cunha earned their chops at the four-star Oakroom at the storied Seelbach Hotel in downtown Louisville. The duo has an upscale touch—the wine list is extensive and reasonably priced, and glassware is thin with a few different styles depending on the varietal you choose.

Gerhardt and Cunha call their style "new Southern cooking," embodied by the likes of a bisque of crawfish, shrimp, and lobster finished with tarragon oil, and salmon poached in nearby Woodford county apple cider, accompanied by toasted barley risotto and a Granny Smith apple demi glace. It's creative, fun, and most importantly, delicious.

Lynn's Paradise Café

984 Barret Ave.
Louisville, Kentucky 40204-2063
502.583.3447
www.lynnsparadisecafe.com

Breakfast and lunch Monday 8 am–2:30 pm; Breakfast, lunch, and dinner Tuesday–Friday 7 am–10 pm, Saturday and Sunday 8 am–10 pm

Breakfast $2.25–$12; Lunch $3.50–$13; Dinner $8–$19

MCC, Full bar

Breakfast served anytime

Lynn's Paradise Café is a destination restaurant for two reasons: the special Bloody Mary cocktails with a half dozen garnishes, and the Kentucky-Fried sculpture garden of cement farm animals and giant tea cups in the parking lot. The atmosphere inside is funky. A large tree with a painted trunk is hung with multiple plastic Easter eggs and serves as the dining room's focal point; tables and chairs are a mismatched collection of garage sale finds. Servers are competent and stylish.

Breakfast is available any time at Lynn's—omelets stuffed with smoked salmon, cream cheese, and capers; thick slabs of cinnamon pecan coffee cake moistened with a ribbon of custard; strong coffee. Lunch adds lots more choices, like the harvest moon chicken salad—chicken fried in walnut oil, chopped and scattered atop pieces of Granny Smith apple, crumbled gorgonzola cheese, and Cajun-spiced pecans on a bed of romaine. You'll find comfort food classics like meatloaf and fried catfish and dinner entrees with upscale flair: spice-rubbed salmon; pan-seared beef tenderloin medallions; and the "grittata," a cheese grits soufflé with Portobello mushrooms, shallots, and roasted red peppers topped with a spicy Creole sauce.

Smith-Berry Winery

855 Drennon Rd. (Highway 202)
New Castle, Kentucky 40050
502.845.7091
www.smithberrywinery.com
smithberrywinery@msn.com

Tuesday–Saturday 10 am–6 pm

This is not a restaurant per se, but a pilgrimage for anyone interested in sustainable agriculture and natural living. The Smith-Berry Winery is owned in part by Mary Berry, the daughter of poet and essayist Wendell Berry, whose influence is stamped on the place. Smith-Berry Winery holds frequent dinners and art exhibitions in addition to its daily wine tastings.

Vietnam Kitchen

5339 Mitscher Ave.
Louisville, Kentucky 40214-2633
502.363.5154

Lunch and dinner weekdays (except Wednesday) 10 am–10 pm, Friday and Saturday 10 am–11 pm. Closed Wednesdays.

Large noodle bowls top out at $8.50

MCC, Beer

Noodle bowls, barbecued tofu in a clay pot, lard naar, shredded pork.

N | North

Anchor Grill

438 Pike St.
Covington, Kentucky 41011-2155
859.431.9498
24 hours seven days a week
$2.50–$9
Cash

Oh, lovers of the greasy spoon, do not miss this place! Anchor Grill is a stellar example of the genre: old linoleum floors, little yellow plastic water glasses, a double Bunn coffee machine constantly rumbling and churning out a steady stream. Anchor Grill is open twenty-four hours and a neon sign in the window says, "We may doze, but never close."

Décor is a high point in the dining room, where each table has its personal jukebox and disco light, and a mirrored ball spins overhead anytime you play a song. The menu is just what it should be: fried eggs slippery with butter, sausage and gravy biscuits, crispy fried goetta, hash browns with onions, and coffee in a white ceramic mug. If you're not in the mood for breakfast, roast beef and mashed potatoes, vegetable beef soup, and grilled cheese are on the menu, too.

Greyhound Tavern

2500 Dixie Highway
Ft. Mitchell, Kentucky 41017-3016
859.331.3767

Dinner Monday–Saturday; Sunday 2 pm–10 pm
First courses $4–$9; Entrees $8.50–$21
MCC, Full bar

Historic and cozy, the Greyhound Tavern is decorated with antiques and plays on its unique heritage: this tavern was once a tea room and popular stopping point in the 1920s for commuters riding streetcars from across the Ohio river in Cincinnati. It's also a great place for comfort food—homemade, sinful mashed potatoes, fried chicken, country ham, and caramel apple pie.

Greyhound Tavern takes pride in its onion rings, which are enormous. A half-order of four is large enough for two people. The wide rings are hard like a crustacean on the outside but just as rewarding on the inside: steamy hot and slippery soft.

Harry's Hometown Diner

6875 Alexandria Pike
Alexandria, Kentucky 41001-1090
859.635.1943
www.harryshometowndiner.com
Lunch and dinner seven days a week
Lunch and dinner $3.99–$7.29
MCC

You can experience the Americana of a lunch counter again, or for the first time, at Harry's Diner. Harry, the owner, stands behind the busy counter at this stainless-steel restaurant shouting orders and compulsively wiping everything down with a little white cloth. He has on wildly patterned pants and occasionally leaves his station to troll the narrow building for children. When he finds one, he tells her she's going to turn into whatever she's eating ("You like chicken nuggets? You're going to turn into one big nugget!") and hands her a baseball card.

Looking around Harry's Diner, one could surmise he's been saving the decorations for his restaurant since the sixties. Along the walls are framed photos of hot-rods, album covers like The Best of the Ink Spots, and vintage Cincinnati Reds paraphernalia. His-and-hers bathrooms are designated with Archie and Betty comic books. Outside, the traditional stainless-steel diner has a landscaped front yard and a gazebo overlooking the parking lot, which Harry shares with a Wal-Mart. An enormous red neon sign on the rooftop makes a nostalgic plea: DINER.

Most customers are regulars, and eyes widen in mock astonishment upon discovering a newcomer. "You mean you're first-timers? Well, let me shake your hand. Hi there, I'm Susan. It's nice to meet you." Susan the server flashes a pretty smile and describes the drinks (chocolate malts, vanilla cokes) and main dishes (liver and onions, tuna salad plate) and then dashes off to pick up another table's order as soon as it hits the heat lamp.

Hofbrauhaus

3rd and Saratoga Streets at Newport on the Levee
Newport, Kentucky 41071
☎ 859.491.7200
www.hofbrauhausnewport.com

🕐 Lunch and dinner Monday–Saturday 11 am–midnight, Sunday noon–10 pm

$ First courses $2.99–$8.99; Sandwiches and salads $6.99–$12.99; Entrees $8.99–$24.99; Desserts $3.99–$5.99

Hofbrauhaus Newport has three areas for merrymaking: a dining room seating one hundred at small, intimate tables; a beer hall with casual, communal tables and a stage for touring Bavarian bands; and outside, a beer garden with a view of the Cincinnati skyline.

A master German butcher prepares much of Hofbrauhaus's menu and it's fair to say this restaurant isn't prime for vegans. It's about meat, baby, and I don't mean chicken. Some of the best dishes include Bierwurst, a deliciously

plump, pink sausage of coarsely ground meat and garlic, and Münchener Grillwurst, a deep red, finely ground Mettwurst heavily spiced with white pepper. There are two types of bratwurst. The first is a bun-size wurst of coarsely ground pork and veal with fresh coriander and nutmeg. This brat is better than the Nürnberger Bratwürstl, a dish of five breakfast-size links, which were over-cooked on my visit. Another good dish is the Kasseler Rippchen, tangy smoked pork chops slightly reminiscent of ham, but with a thicker, meatier texture.

Roasted pork shank with crackling skin called Schweinshaxe Münchener is delightful served very hot, but if the dish cools it can turn unappealingly gummy. Emphasize to the server you'd like your roasted pork shank straight from the oven and you'll be sure to enjoy Schweinshaxe Münchener at its primeval best.

MARGARITA'S

3218 Dixie Highway
Erlanger, Kentucky 41018-1828
☎ 859.426.9792

Lunch and dinner seven days a week

$ Entrees $8–$13

★ MCC, Full bar

! Children's menu, multiple locations

Classic Mexican food: chicken flautas, fajitas, enchiladas, chiles rellenos.

Tousey House

5963 North Jefferson St.
Burlington, Kentucky 41005-9596

- 859.689.0200
- Dinner Thursday–Saturday 5:30 pm–10 pm
- Prix fixe menu is $35
- MCC, Full bar
- Call ahead to reserve a table

Tousey House is an eclectic, stylish restaurant that sits across from the Boone County court house in the county seat of Burlington. Burlington was founded in 1799 as Craig's Camp, named after a local landowner, and it's always been smallish—in 1986, Burlington had a population of six hundred. The sense of Burlington as a small town is so definitive that you might find it downright odd to happen upon Tousey House, with its three chefs in the kitchen and important regional fare.

Boone County's countryside is growing, and this explains, in part, why Tousey House is where it is. Yet while the pasturelands of Burlington and its neighbors are cut into subdivisions, Tousey House owner and chef Kristy Schalck (rhymes with chalk) digs her heels deep into preserving the foundation of Kentucky cooking.

Entrees range from beef tenderloin to southern game birds like quail to Chilean sea bass. Each dish is prepared with sophistication and features local Kentucky ingredients, like the beef tenderloin accompanied by a Kentucky roots cake. The roots—purple Peruvian and Yukon gold potatoes, carrot, roasted garlic—remain intact as tender, chunky pieces, molded and fried together. Such heavy pieces fall apart as you break the cake with your fork, each bit a warm, crispy, slightly sweet surprise.

York Street Café

738 York St.
Newport, Kentucky 41071
859.261.9675
www.yorkstonline.com
terry@yorkstonline.com

Lunch Tuesday–Saturday; Dinner Tuesday–Sunday

Salads $9–$17; First courses $5–$10; Entrees $13–$25

MCC, Full bar

York Street Café is a combination of restaurant, café, art gallery, and bar with live bands, each separated by a flight of stairs in this Queen Anne-style building dating from the 1880s.

On the first floor, the restaurant serves casual hipster fare like hummus and tabbouleh platters, but also has trendier fare like Asian lettuce wraps and upscale entrees like pan-seared scallops with truffle butter and filet mignon with port reduction and gorgonzola cheese. The wine list is solid and desserts de rigueur—you could be happy here just with a fat wedge of layer cake and cappuccino in the back garden patio.

Live music starts around nine on the second floor, and an art gallery on the third floor showcases local artists.

SW | Southwest

Bon Ton Mini Mart

2036 Madison St.
Henderson, Kentucky 42420-4568
☎ 270.826.1207

Breakfast, lunch, and dinner Monday–Friday 4 am–7 pm; Breakfast and lunch Saturday 4 am–3 pm

Half-chicken basket $6.31; Chicken breast $2.12; Wings and thighs $1.06

Cash only

This small restaurant is no longer a mart, it's a Mecca to fried chicken. Thick-battered, spicy, and spitting hot, favorite accompaniments are hand-rolled biscuits and country-fried apples.

George's

1346 E. 4th St.
Owensboro, Kentucky 42303-0130
☎ 270.926.9276

Breakfast, lunch, and dinner Monday–Saturday 8 am–8 pm

$2.40–$8.50

MCC, Beer

Barbecued mutton, beef brisket, pork, and chicken, plus burgoo.

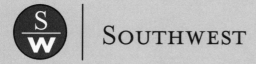

Moonlite Bar-B-Q

2840 W. Parrish Ave.
Owensboro, Kentucky 42301-2689
270.684.8143
www.moonlite.com

Monday–Thursday 9 am–9 pm, Friday and Saturday 9 am–9:30 pm, Sunday 10 am–3 pm

Barbecue dinners $6.25–$10.25 including two sides; Shrimp dinner $9.45; Sandwiches $2.50–$4.70

MCC, Beer and wine

Moonlite Bar-B-Q is best known for their barbecued mutton, which you can get on a sandwich or as a platter. They also serve burgoo, salads, catfish, and grilled cheese for the unadventurous diner. Desserts like pecan pie and peanut butter pie are on the menu, too.

C | Central

Darlin' Jean's Apple Cobbler Café

107 E. Main St.
Midway, Kentucky 40347
859.846.9485
Lunch Monday–Saturday 11 am–2 pm; Dinner Thursday and Friday 5 pm–9 pm
Pizza $3–$15; Sandwiches $5.50–$6.50
Cash

Darlin' Jean's is the lunchtime hangout in Midway offering pizzas and sandwiches. If you're looking for breakfast in this area, you might want to try her other spot: Darlin' Jean's Country Store Café, 4000 Leestown Rd., 859.243.0038. They're open for breakfast and lunch Monday–Saturday 6:30 am–3 pm.

Holly Hill Inn

426 N. Winter St.
Midway, Kentucky 40347
859.846.4732
Dinner Wednesday–Saturday 5:30 pm–9 pm; Brunch Sunday noon–2:30 pm
Three-course meal $35 per person; Three-course wine pairing $18
MCC, Full bar
Reservations recommended

Holly Hill's chef, native Kentuckian Ouita Michel, rubs elbows with culinary inspirations like Alice Waters and uses fresh, locally produced seasonal ingredients. Chris Michel, who like his wife is a Culinary Institute of America (CIA) grad, is slogging his way through the rigorous tests to become a master sommelier, of which there are only fifty-six in the U.S. and none in Kentucky.

Lanterns illuminate the front porch of the 1839 Greek Revival mansion that houses their restaurant. Holly Hill's three dining rooms seat sixty-five people at white-clothed tables. Gleaming silverware and lovely stemware lend a rarified charm, and hand-spun ceramic chargers make it feel very Kentucky. The prix fixe menu offers a choice of three first courses and six entrees, plus a lengthy dessert menu. The Michels change their menu frequently and are inspired by themes such as New Orleans French, embodied by oysters wrapped in buckwheat crepes with caviar and country ham; frog legs in crystal butter; and duck, andouille, and oyster gumbo.

Elmwood breast of game hen Rochembeau, a flavorful, tender, and crisp breast of hen with béarnaise and Marchands de vin sauce, was unspeakably perfect the night I dined here. Cast-iron skillet blackened Green River New York Strip was red, thick, juicy, tender, and might I add, huge? It was paired with a petite lump crab cake and whiskey sauce. Desserts are hardly an afterthought; sweet-toothed diners should make a pilgrimage here for the chocolate truffle torte with caramel nuts and vanilla bean cream.

The small town of Midway, Kentucky, is filled with good antique shops, and the itinerary of a longer stay could quickly fill with shopping down the main thoroughfare, Railroad Street. The Michels say a visit wouldn't be complete without a trip to nearby Woodford Reserve Distillery (859/879-1812) and the Smith-Berry Winery (502/845-7091). Both are within an hour's drive and offer tours and tastings.

Loudon Square Buffet

801 N. Broadway
Lexington, Kentucky 40508-1591

☎ 859.252.9741

🕘 Lunch and dinner seven days a week

$ Buffet $6 for adults, $3.75 for children

★ Cash only

Comfort-food-o-rama! This buffet has fried fish, chicken, roast beef, green beans, mashed potatoes, pie, cobbler, and pudding. And lots of other stuff, too.

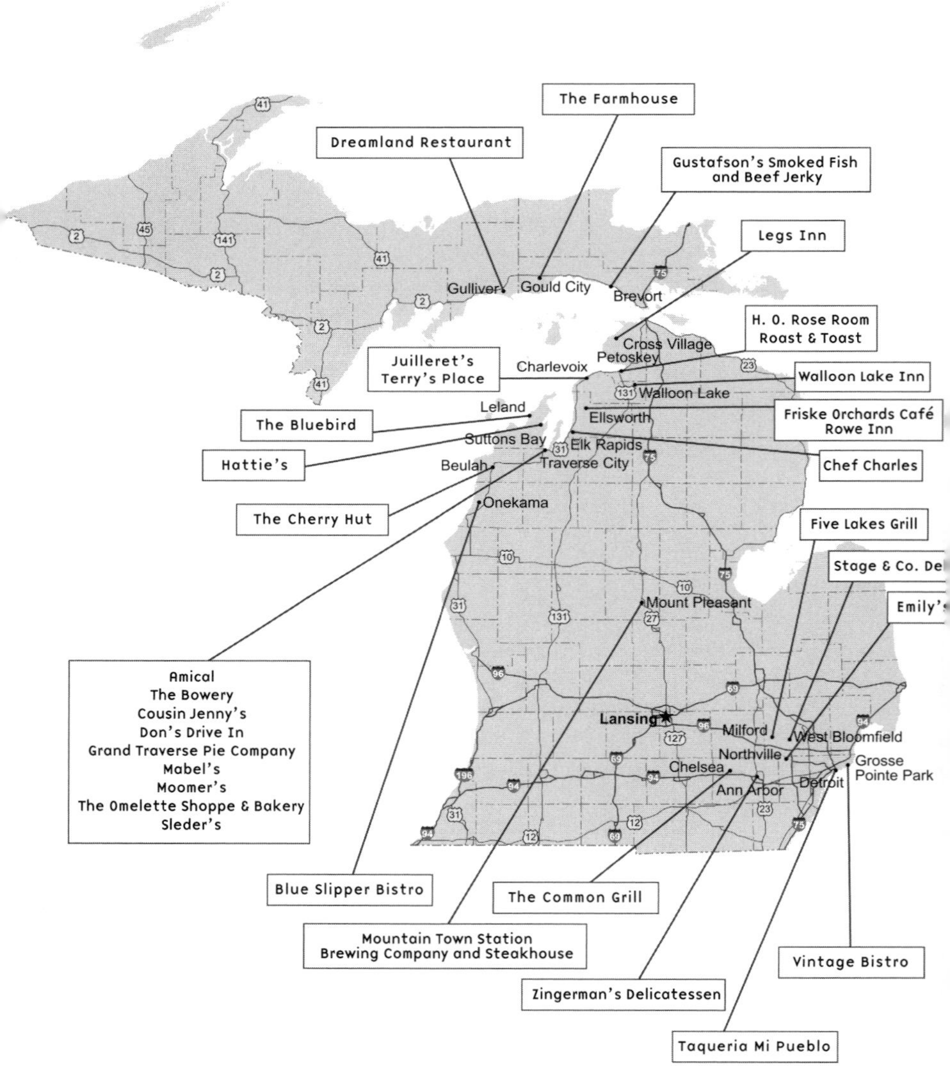

The Farmhouse
Dreamland Restaurant
Gustafson’s Smoked Fish and Beef Jerky
Legs Inn
H. O. Rose Room
Roast & Toast
Juilleret’s
Terry’s Place
Walloon Lake Inn
Friske Orchards Café
Rowe Inn
The Bluebird
Hattie’s
Chef Charles
The Cherry Hut
Five Lakes Grill
Stage & Co. De
Emily’
Amical
The Bowery
Cousin Jenny’s
Don’s Drive In
Grand Traverse Pie Company
Mabel’s
Moomer’s
The Omelette Shoppe & Bakery
Sleder’s
Blue Slipper Bistro
The Common Grill
Mountain Town Station Brewing Company and Steakhouse
Vintage Bistro
Zingerman’s Delicatessen
Taqueria Mi Pueblo
Gulliver
Gould City
Brevort
Cross Village
Petoskey
Charlevoix
Walloon Lake
Leland
Ellsworth
Suttons Bay
Elk Rapids
Beulah
Traverse City
Onekama
Mount Pleasant
Lansing
Milford
West Bloomfield
Northville
Chelsea
Ann Arbor
Detroit
Grosse Pointe Park

MICHIGAN

Michigan is a lovely state for vacationing, and after returning from a trip here, it's easy to feel slightly smug and nationalistic. Why bother traveling abroad when you have all these fabulous bistros, crystal lakes, white sand beaches, and fresh fish? Michigan is so above-board American! Well ... there's no need to be provincial. Europe has its place on any food lover's itinerary, but Michigan is a fabulous food destination, and that's the point.

Detroit has any number of fine dining establishments (see below or try Jeremy in Keego Harbor 248.681.2124 or Tribute 248.848.9393), but I headed straight for Mexicantown, to Taqueria Mi Pueblo for a savory round of tacos stuffed with chorizo dripping with spicy red oil.

In Ann Arbor, Zingerman's Deli is a maze of temptation, and it's worth succumbing to the thick, juicy layers of sliced corned beef piled onto soft and tender bread with wickedly crispy crust. The contrast between the center and crunchy edges of this bread embodies the phrase, "God is in all things." Vegetarians visiting Ann Arbor should try Seva (734.662.1111).

Some of my favorite breakfasts were up north, where starting the day with as many calories as possible seems to be the unstated goal. A cinnamon bun at The Farmhouse in the Upper Peninsula is still on my mind months later: A ribbon of slightly sweet, warm, yeast-fed dough wrapped around cinnamon, sugar, and butter, the roll overwhelmed its medium-size plate. As I cut it in thirds to share it with my daughters, streams of sugar frosting ran over my fingers. Pillsbury will never be the same again.

In the south, visitors to the Bavarian-style town of Frankenmuth looking for comfort food should try Zehnder's family-style chicken dinners with all the fixings (800.863.7999). Frankenmuth is famous for its charming shops, but really, Zehnder's is something to see: it seats fifteen hundred people in a single dining room and claims to be the nation's largest family-owned restaurant.

Northwest

Amical

229 E. Front St.
Traverse City, Michigan 49684
231.941.8888
www.amical.com

Lunch and dinner Monday–Saturday 11 am–10 pm; Sunday brunch 9 am–3 pm and light menu 3 pm–5 pm

Lunch $10; Dinner $10–$30

MCC, Full bar

Creative bistro fare with a French accent. Expect to find homemade pastries alongside entrees like braised short ribs and filet of beef in morel mushroom sauce.

Blue Slipper Bistro

8058 First St.
Onekama, Michigan 49675
231.889.4045

Lunch and dinner Tuesday–Thursday 11:30 am–8:30 pm, Friday and Saturday 11:30 am–9:30 pm, Sunday noon–8:30 pm. Closed Mondays.

Dinner $8–$20

MCC, Full bar

The menu ranges from sandwiches to large salads at lunch plus upscale items like veal scaloppine saltimbocca and pasta dishes for dinner.

The Bluebird

102 E. River St.
Leland, Michigan 49654
231.256.9081
www.leelanau.com/bluebird

Lunch and dinner Monday–Saturday 11:30 am–9:30 pm; Brunch Sunday 10 am–2 pm

Lunch sandwiches $4–$7; Dinner first courses $5–$7; Entrees $15–$22

MCC, Full bar

Fried whitefish dinner, cinnamon buns. Changing menu selections. Also international theme nights such as Thai and Italian.

The Bowery

13512 Peninsula Dr.
Traverse City, Michigan 49684
231.223.4333
www.michiganmenu.com

Dinner Sunday–Thursday 5 pm–9 pm, Friday and Saturday 5 pm–10 pm

Sandwiches $8; First courses $4.25–$8; Entrees $12.75–$18

MCC, Full bar

Summer hours are Sunday–Thursday 4 pm–10 pm, Friday and Saturday 4 pm–11 pm

The Bowery is the casual sister restaurant of Bower's Harbor Inn, a beautiful 1880s summer home turned fine-dining destination on the Old Mission Peninsula in Traverse City. The peninsula has a unique microclimate—it's very warm with sandy soil and an extended growing season compared to other parts of northern Michigan—which enables The Bowery's owners to maintain an extensive garden and vineyards. The Bowery makes its own wines, some of them award-winning, and the garden is a pretty place for a walk before dinner.

Unlike the Bower's Harbor Inn, a fancy restaurant that shares the building and faces the harbor, The Bowery is family-friendly and casual enough for jeans. Located behind the Bower's Harbor

Inn, The Bowery's interior has one large dining room plus a loft for private parties and an open kitchen. Menu highlights are the smoked Whitefish dip, creamy and subtle, served with crunchy lavash chips; and the cherry chicken salad, loaded with dried Michigan cherries and tossed with a not-too-sweet vinaigrette.

Mess O'Perch is a plateful of hot, moist local fish, lightly breaded and fried. On the night I visited, the perch tasted like it was caught only hours before. Also a hit was the hickory rotisserie chicken, in a tangy, flavorful marinade and served with crisp, steamed veggies.

Chef Charles

147 River St.
Elk Rapids, Michigan 49629
☎ 231.264.8901

🕘 Lunch and dinner Monday–Saturday 11 am–8 pm, Sunday 12 pm–8 pm

$ Sandwiches $1.50; Large specialty pizza $16

★ MCC

This is a no-frills pizza place in a key location for those hitting the road driving north. Located on the main commercial thoroughfare of smalltown Elk Rapids, Chef Charles sells its pizzas by the slice through a take-out window. One slice and a small drink is $2.12 (and the small drink is a must—it's a package deal).

The Cherry Hut

216 N. Michigan Ave. (US 31)
Beulah, Michigan 49617

☎ 231.882.4431

🕒 Lunch and dinner seven days a week 10 am–10 pm. Open seasonally, call ahead for dates.

$ $3–$15

★ MCC

The Cherry Hut uses local cherries in homemade baked goods such as sour cherry muffins and cherry pie made from a recipe used since 1922. Fresh roast chicken everyday, cherry chicken salad, specialty salads, and sandwiches are also on the menu. Breakfast buffet on weekends.

Cousin Jenny's

129 S. Union St.
Traverse City, Michigan 49684

☎ 231.941.7821

🕒 Breakfast and lunch Monday–Friday 7 am–6pm, Saturday 7 am–5 pm. Closed Sunday.

$ $4–$10

★ MCC

Northern Michigan is a melting pot of Italian, Polish, and Cornish immigrant populations who came to work as miners in the iron-rich Menominee Range starting in the late 1800s. Cousin Jenny's Cornish Pasties (that's paastys) is one of the great culinary remainders of that influx.

This bright, casual breakfast and lunch spot sells handheld pastries similar in constitution to pot pies, filled with savory combinations of meat and vegetables. The most traditional is the steak pastie, with beef, potatoes, onion, rutabaga, and herbs. You hold the pastie in one hand and dip it into either gravy or sour cream or both before each bite. This isn't too dainty a process; some choose to sit down and eat their pasties with knife and fork.

Pasties are a perfect fast food—neatly packaged in their own pastry wrapper—and it's a shame they aren't more readily available outside northern Michigan. Cousin Jenny's also offers a dozen or so salads, breakfast bobbys (pasties filled with sausage and egg, etc.), and desserts baked in-house.

Don's Drive In

2030 US 31 N.
Traverse City, Michigan 49684
231.938.1860

Lunch and dinner seven days a week 10:30 am–9:30 pm

$5–$10

Cash

Three big decisions to make at Don's Drive In: To eat in the car or inside at a table (this is, after all, a traditional drive-in). To order the regular quarter-pound burger or the Big D (that's a half-pound of beautiful char-grilled beef to you). And third—well, it isn't really a decision. It's self-evident that given the choice between a malt flavored with cherry syrup or a malt made with real Michigan cherries, you'd wisely opt for the fresh fruit.

Grand Traverse Pie Company

525 West Front St.
Traverse City, Michigan 49684
231.922.7437
www.gtpie.com

Breakfast and lunch Monday–Friday 9 am–6 pm, Saturday 9 am–5 pm

Pies $4–$6

MCC

Multiple locations

A cute, cozy shop specializing in homemade pies, this location was the first of what's now a crust-wielding empire with multiple locations. It's popular for a reason and that reason is pie, baby, and I don't mean frozen. Cherry pie, apple pie, chicken pot pie … expect to choose from about a dozen. You can also get an espresso or smoothie here, plus sandwiches and salads.

Hattie's

111 St. Joseph St.
Suttons Bay, Michigan 49682
231.271.6222
www.hatties.com

Dinner Tuesday–Saturday 5:30 pm–9:30 pm. Closed Sunday and Monday.

$24–$33

MCC, Full bar

With white tablecloths and a wine list that has been recognized by *Wine Spectator* magazine, Hattie's is among the handful of restaurants in northern Michigan serving a discerning crowd. The menu changes weekly and uses local ingredients, such as sautéed walleye in garlic cream and rack of venison with tart cherry sauce. Set three-course dinners are available some nights, as are early bird specials.

Mabel's

472 Munson
Traverse City, Michigan 49684
231.947.0252

Breakfast, lunch, and dinner seven days a week 7 am–11 pm

$4–$13

MCC

Mabel's combines family dining and American comfort food classics. Breakfast is available all day, and the menu always lists two homemade soups a day plus buttermilk-dipped fried chicken, pot roast, and pasta specials.

Moomer's

7263 N. Long Lake Rd.
Traverse City, Michigan 49684
231.941.4122
www.moomers.com

June–August seven days a week noon–10 pm; Fall and Spring Tuesday–Sunday noon–9 pm; Winter Friday and Saturday noon–9 pm

$2–$6

Cash

Seasonal hours, call first

Homemade ice cream shop featuring brownie sundaes, cowpie ice cream sandwiches, and frozen yogurt.

The Omelette Shoppe & Bakery

1209 E. Front St.
Traverse City, Michigan 49686
231.946.0590

Breakfast and lunch

Omelets $6.60–$7; Pancakes and waffles $2–$4; Sandwiches $5.29–$6

MCC

Second location—124 Cass St., 231.946.0912

The Omelette Shoppe & Bakery has one of the most complete omelet menus I've seen, including a classic French method omelet, light and fluffy with just a sprinkle of salt, and seven kinds of frittata. Eggs benedict are lovely, with a creamy, thick hollandaise that seemed made to order. Other good breakfasts to try are the multigrain pancakes made with nutty-flavored flour and studded with

sunflower seeds and walnuts, and the French toast featuring house-made oat bran cherry pecan bread.

Lunches in this non-smoking, sunny spot range from big burgers to a vegetarian sandwich on multigrain bread with pesto, havarti, cucumbers, and sprouts. This being northern Michigan, dried cherries find their way into a lot of dishes, including the chicken salad and cherry-pecan sausage.

The one-room restaurant is lined with booths. It's no frills but pleasant, with families, retirees, and folks on their way to work all crowded in to enjoy a coveted, favorite breakfast. You pay at the counter on the way out, and I noticed smart customers picking up their orders of a dozen cinnamon rolls before walking through the door.

Sleder's

717 Randolph St.
Traverse City, Michigan 49684
231.947.9213
www.sleders.com

Lunch and dinner Monday–Thursday 11 am–10 pm, Friday and Saturday 11 am–11 pm, Sundays noon–9 pm

$8–$15

MCC, Full bar

A one-hundred-year tradition in Traverse City, Sleder's serves buckets of fried whitefish and Canadian smelt, and it was voted best fish fry in town. This family-friendly spot also serves roasted chicken, buffalo burgers, and burritos.

UPPER PENINSULA

DREAMLAND RESTAURANT

1520 W. US Highway 2
Gulliver, Michigan 49840
906.283.3122

Breakfast, lunch, and dinner seven days a week 7 am–9 pm April through November

Breakfast $2.75–$5.90; Sandwiches $2–$3.25; Entrees $5–$14

MCC

Open seasonally

Dreamland Restaurant bakes its own breads, pies, pasties, and donuts. It's no frills, as is just about every place in the Upper Peninsula, and caters to hunters.

THE FARMHOUSE

W. 17838 US Highway 2
Gould City, Michigan 49838
906.477.6287

Breakfast, lunch, and dinner Sunday–Thursday 7 am–9 pm, Friday and Saturday 7 am–10 pm

Breakfast $3–$10; Lunch and dinner $7–$28

MCC, Full bar

The Farmhouse sits in a newly built log cabin fronting an Upper Peninsula-style recreation development with miniature golf, stocked trout ponds, cabins, and a snowmobile trail. The restaurant is a center of activity both for vacationers traversing

Highway 2 across the southern U.P., and locals. They all come for the cozy wood-beam and stone interior, and the home-style food.

Breakfast bestsellers are large, tender cinnamon rolls drizzled with sweet frosting, and sausage gravy on biscuits. Studded with dime-size chunks of sausage crisp from the frying pan, the gravy is rich with cream and flecked with red pepper flakes. Corned beef hash is homemade here, made of shredded, savory brisket and thinly sliced golden fried potatoes.

For lunch, owner Fred Burton says his pasties (meat and potato-filled pastries) smothered in gravy are big enough for two. Dinner ranges from fried chicken to T-bone steaks and trout caught in the ponds outside.

Gustafson's Smoked Fish and Beef Jerky

4321 West US 2
Brevort, Michigan 49760

906.292.5424

Seven days a week 8 am–6 pm

Jerky $15 per pound; Smoked fish $23 per pound

MCC

Note to all jerky fans: don't miss this place. Gustafson's is a gas station, and I guess you can't really call it a restaurant—unless you like to make a meal out of jerky. In which case: they make their own, including beef and buffalo jerky and smoked fish (jerky's white meat) including whitefish, salmon, and trout.

N | NORTH (lower peninsula)

FRISKE ORCHARDS CAFE

10743 N. US 31
Ellsworth, Michigan 49729
231.599.2604
www.friske.com

Breakfast and lunch 8 am–3 pm

$2–$6

MCC

Friske Orchards is a third-generation, family-owned orchard where you can pick your own apples and berries before sitting down to a casual, wholesome lunch in the café. Early risers know to buy a dozen of Friske's fabulous cherry donuts; stoked with the essence of fresh Michigan cherries, there's nothing else like them.

H.O. ROSE ROOM AT STAFFORD'S PERRY HOTEL

Bay & Lewis Sts.
Petoskey, Michigan 49770
231.347.2516

Lunch Monday–Friday 11 am–2 pm; Dinner Tuesday–Saturday 7 pm–10:30 pm

Dinner entrees $18–$25

MCC, Full bar

A formal restaurant in an elegant old hotel, the H.O. Rose Room menu lists entrees such as tangerine sage chicken and caraway roasted rack of lamb, plus daily specials like pork medallions sautéed with pear and cherries in apple cider cream sauce. A cellar at Stafford's Perry Hotel offers more casual fare, including fried whitefish and sandwiches.

Juilleret's

1418 Bridge St.
Charlevoix, Michigan 49720
231.547.9212

Breakfast and lunch seven days a week
5:30 am–3 pm

Breakfast $2–$8; Lunch $4–$14.50

MCC

A breakfast and lunch staple, Juilleret's bakes its own breads and rolls. Specialties include cinnamon French toast, raspberry pancakes, and pure Michigan maple syrup sundaes.

Legs Inn

6425 Lakeshore Dr.
Cross Village, Michigan 49723
231.526.2281
www.legsinn.com

Lunch and dinner seven days a week

Lunch $6–$10; Dinner first courses $4–$9;
Entrees $11–$19

MCC, Full bar

Open seasonally May 21–October 17

Located on a bluff overlooking Lake Michigan, Legs Inn is a stone lodge with a fantastic interior showcasing wood sculpture and Native American artwork. The founder of this family-owned restaurant, Stanley Smolak, was born in Poland and the menu is largely Polish, offering pierogis and Polish dumplings and sausages, plus more mainstream American fare like steaks and pork chops. Legs Inn also has a stellar beer list, with more than one hundred kinds of beer from around the world.

Roast & Toast

309 E. Lake St.
Petoskey, Michigan 49770
231.347.7767
www.roastandtoast.com

Breakfast, lunch, and dinner Monday–Thursday 7 am–7 pm, Friday–Sunday 7 am–8 pm

$4–$10

MCC

This friendly, casual spot serves freshly roasted coffee, home-made muffins, soups, and chicken pot pie.

Rowe Inn

6303 E. Jordan Rd. (County Road C48)
Ellsworth, Michigan 49729
231.588.7351

Dinner seven days a week 6 pm–8 pm

$19–$36

MCC, Full bar

Reservations required, notable wine list

Midwestern food-lovers consider the journey to the remote Rowe Inn as a kind of culinary pilgrimage. The French Provencal menu may include first courses such as pecan-stuffed morel mushrooms and venison sausage with green lentils and entrees like sautéed veal with morel bordelaise and rack of lamb with mustard cream. Rowe Inn's more casual sister restaurant Bistro Bridgette offers terrines, French onion soup, and tartines.

Terry's Place

112 Antrim St.
Charlevoix, Michigan 49720
☎ 231.547.2799

🕘 Dinner Tuesday–Sunday 5 pm–9 pm, Friday and Saturday 5 pm–10 pm. Closed Mondays.

$ $18-$30

★ MCC, Full bar

An intimate restaurant in a small, upstairs location with white tablecloths, Terry's offers fresh lake fish, plus veal, steaks, and duck.

Walloon Lake Inn

4178 West St.
Walloon Lake Village, Michigan 49796
☎ 231.535.2999
www.walloonlakeinn.com

🕘 Dinner seven days a week 6 pm–10 pm

$ $20–$25

★ MCC, Full bar

! Reservations required

Located on charming Walloon Lake, this one-hundred-year-old bed and breakfast doubles as a restaurant and cooking school. Fresh fish specials, including ruby trout and pumpkin-seed crusted whitefish, partner with pastas, veal, and filet mignon.

Southeast

The Common Grill

112 S. Main St.
Chelsea, Michigan 48118
734.475.0470
www.commongrill.com

Lunch and dinner Tuesday 11 am–10 pm, Wednesday and Thursday 11 am–10:30 pm, Friday and Saturday 11 am–11 pm, Sunday 11 am–9 pm

Salads and sandwiches $4–$13; First courses $4–$12; Entrees $17–$26

MCC, Full bar

Call ahead for a table

This charming bistro on the main thoroughfare of Chelsea reveals the influence discerning suburbanites can have on small town America. The restaurant's tall window panes look out onto a restored shopping district in a bedroom community of Ann Arbor and the outer reaches of Detroit. Inside, it's semi-casual; most patrons raise the dress code a notch above jeans.

Owned by chef and namesake Craig Common, Common Grill was listed by *Bon Appetit* as a top neighborhood restaurant in the US, with dishes like the grilled flat-iron steak fingered as standouts. The steak is topped with a zinfandel reduction and blue-cheese walnut butter, alongside white cheddar mashed potatoes and crisp, sautéed vegetables.

First courses include creamy, dense roasted parmesan custard with grilled flatbread, roasted three-onion soup, and lobster spring rolls with Asian slaw and Chinese mustard sauce. For dessert, homemade cream puffs are filled with mocha chip ice cream, topped with warm bittersweet chocolate sauce and sprinkled with candied almonds. It all adds up to more love in the world.

Emily's

505 North Center St.
Northville, Michigan 48167
☎ 428.349.0505
www.emilysrestaurant.com

Dinner Tuesday–Saturday beginning at 5:30 pm

First courses $5.50–$18; Entrees $24–$39

MCC, Full bar

Reservations recommended

Set in a quaint Victorian cottage, Emily's cuisine is anything but demure. Chef Rick Halberg is a graduate of the Culinary Institute of America and has cooked for the James Beard Foundation. Here, his seasonal French-Mediterranean menu features fennel-cured salmon with mustard crème fraiche and blood oranges, and a filet of beef with oxtail and barley, heirloom carrots, haricot verts, and a cabernet-beef reduction.

Five Lakes Grill

424 North Main St.
Milford, Michigan 48381
☎ 248.684.7455
www.fivelakesgrill.com

Dinner Tuesday–Thursday 4 pm–10 pm, Friday and Saturday 4 pm–11 pm

First courses $4–$12; Entrees $15.50–$30

MCC, Full bar

Reservations recommended

You may recognize chef Brian Polcyn as the subject of the book *The Soul of a Chef* by Michael Ruhlman, which chronicled the chef's pursuit of the coveted Certified Master Chef degree. But at Polcyn's casual yet refined Five Lakes Grill, the chef turns the focus away from himself and onto regional, sensational food. Polcyn is known for dishes like potato-crusted Lake Superior whitefish with rock shrimp mousseline and shrimp cognac sauce, as well as his charcuterie—notably the first course farmer's plate of housemade charcuterie selections with German potato salad.

Stage & Co. Deli

6073 Orchard Lake Rd.
West Bloomfield Hills, Michigan 48322
248.855.6622

Brunch, lunch, and dinner Tuesday–Thursday 10 am–10 pm, Friday 10 am–11 pm, Saturday 9 am–11 pm and Sunday 9 am–9 pm

Sandwiches $7–$11, Salads $6–$12, Entrees $10–$16

MCC, Full bar

Regulars refer to this traditional New York-style delicatessen as "Stage." But ask about their favorite offering on the laundry-list menu, and these regulars are less concise: "Sweet and Sour trout, the hot rye bread, cheese blintz, roast turkey off the bone, blueberry pancakes, the #32, that's a corned beef, coleslaw, Russian dressing, and imported Swiss on rye—seedless rye." Alright, alright! Enough already!

The restaurant is spacious and inviting. A well-trained staff trolls the room, water pitcher in one hand and cleaning cloth in the other. Servers are solicitous, setting out platters of pickles and making way for more and more plates of homemade goodies like strawberry shortcake to follow chicken salad and flaky pot pie.

Along the walls are the de rigueur black and white photos of Hollywood stars from the golden era (the restaurant's name, Stage, refers to theatrical performance) and in front is a long deli case doing a brisk takeout business—which is the real star of the show.

Taqueria Mi Pueblo

7278 Dix St.
Detroit, Michigan 48209-1204
313.841.3315

Breakfast, lunch, and dinner Sunday–Friday 9 am–11 pm, Saturday 9 am–midnight

Breakfast $4.25–$5.75; Tacos $2 each; Super burros $7.50; Soups $7–$9

MCC

When owner Jose Lopez bought an empty, century-old building in the heart of Detroit's Mexicantown, few people saw the potential for a restaurant. At first, Lopez could only fit forty-five diners at a time—not accommodations for a restaurant empire. But in the case of Taqueria Mi Pueblo, Lopez's vision for the future made all the difference.

Lopez renovated the building, tripled the seating capacity, and added lovely murals, terra cotta tile, and other Mexican ceramics to give his restaurant an artsy, more refined air. And then, he asked his sisters to cook. What a smart move!

A plate of three tacos arrives with each taco layered with two soft, corn tortillas and filled with a choice of chorizo, marinated pork, chicken, or various other more adventurous animal parts (pig stomach and beef head, for example). The chorizo is amazingly good, sprinkled with minced onions and cilantro . . . but really, the pork might be better. Not that the chicken is bad—it is very good too. So get a platter, served with whipped refried beans and light-as-air fluffy Mexican rice studded with chunks of fresh tomato and poblano chile pepper.

Vintage Bistro

18450 Mack Ave.
Grosse Point Farms, Michigan 48236
313.886.9950

Dinner Monday–Thursday 5 pm–10 pm, Friday and Saturday 5 pm–10:30 pm

First courses $4–$10.75; Entrees $10–$24

MCC, Full bar

Vintage Bistro may appear old-fashioned—housed in a German Tudor building and with tables decked in checked tablecloths—but don't be fooled. The menu is entirely up-to-date. Chefs Christian Borden and Jon-Louis Seavitt pair pan-roasted pheasant and crepes stuffed with Anaheim peppers and goat cheese. A pork tenderloin is served with grilled persimmon and black cherry essence. There's more than a little French influence here, but it combines with twenty-first-century American style (think homemade potato chips with blue cheese sauce) for that wonderfully authentic gem found all over the Midwest nowadays: the contemporary American bistro.

Zingerman's Delicatessen

422 Detroit St.
Ann Arbor, Michigan 48104-1118
734.663.3354
www.zingermans.com

Breakfast, lunch, and dinner seven days a week 7 am–10 pm

Breakfast $2–$11; Sandwiches $7.50–$12; Salads $6–$11; Desserts $2.50–$6

MCC

Zingerman's is a fun, funky deli with personality to burn. In addition to a busy deli case replete with dozens of salads and knishes (my favorite was a red-skinned potato salad in roasted red pepper dressing), a bake house next door bakes unique, artisan breads with natural starters. Try the tsitsel rye—a round rye loaf made with rye flour—and the chocolate cherry bread (which must be on the menu in heaven). You can also buy gourmet items in the store fronting the deli—balsamic vinegars aged in juniper wood and grassy, fresh Petraia olive oil by producer Elia Pellegrino.

The décor is heavy on the fun-loving college town style (Zingerman's shares its hometown with the University of Michigan) with hand-written signs promoting dozens of sandwiches and cold salads. An outdoor eating area with picnic tables and umbrellas has a play area for kids, and the staff brings sandwiches to you. We asked to have our sandwiches cut into fourths (the two sizes, called nosher and fresser, are big and bigger) and the young, friendly deli help were happy to oblige.

Zingerman's uses Angus beef and free-range chicken, and you'll find this to be kind of a pricey place for sandwiches. But the quality of the food and the portion sizes make it worth the extra few dollars.

C | CENTRAL

MOUNTAIN TOWN STATION BREWING COMPANY AND STEAKHOUSE

506 W. Broadway
Mount Pleasant, Michigan 48858
989.775.2337
www.mountaintown.com

Dinner Monday–Thursday 4 pm–10 pm; Lunch and dinner Friday and Saturday 11:30 am–11 pm, Sunday 11:30 am–9 pm

Sandwiches $6–$8; Soups and salads $3.25–$4.25; First courses $4–$10; Entrees $8–$30

MCC, Full bar

In a renovated depot with still-functioning tracks nearby (used by the restaurant's dinner train), Mountain Town Station is part brewery, part family restaurant, and part neighborhood grill. Of the nine types of beer made on the premises, the Iron Horse IPA is most striking, with a bitter, hoppy taste (this one won first place for best India Pale Ale in the 2000 Midwest Beer Fest). Mountain Town Station offers a fun, six-beer sampler (with miniature glasses) so you can compare the flavors of their homemade brews.

The menu is large with about seventy items. Starters include a wild mushroom bisque and white cheddar ale soup, plus the Mountain Town Salad: mixed greens with Granny Smith apples, dried cherries, and chopped walnuts tossed in a maple vinaigrette dressing.

Entrees are strongest in the meat department: St. Louis-style pork ribs, meatloaf with gravy, and bone-in rib eye steak. Two lake fish also grace the menu—herb-pecan crusted fresh walleye drizzled with maple remoulade, and pure and simple broiled Whitefish from Lake Superior—thick, white, and tender.

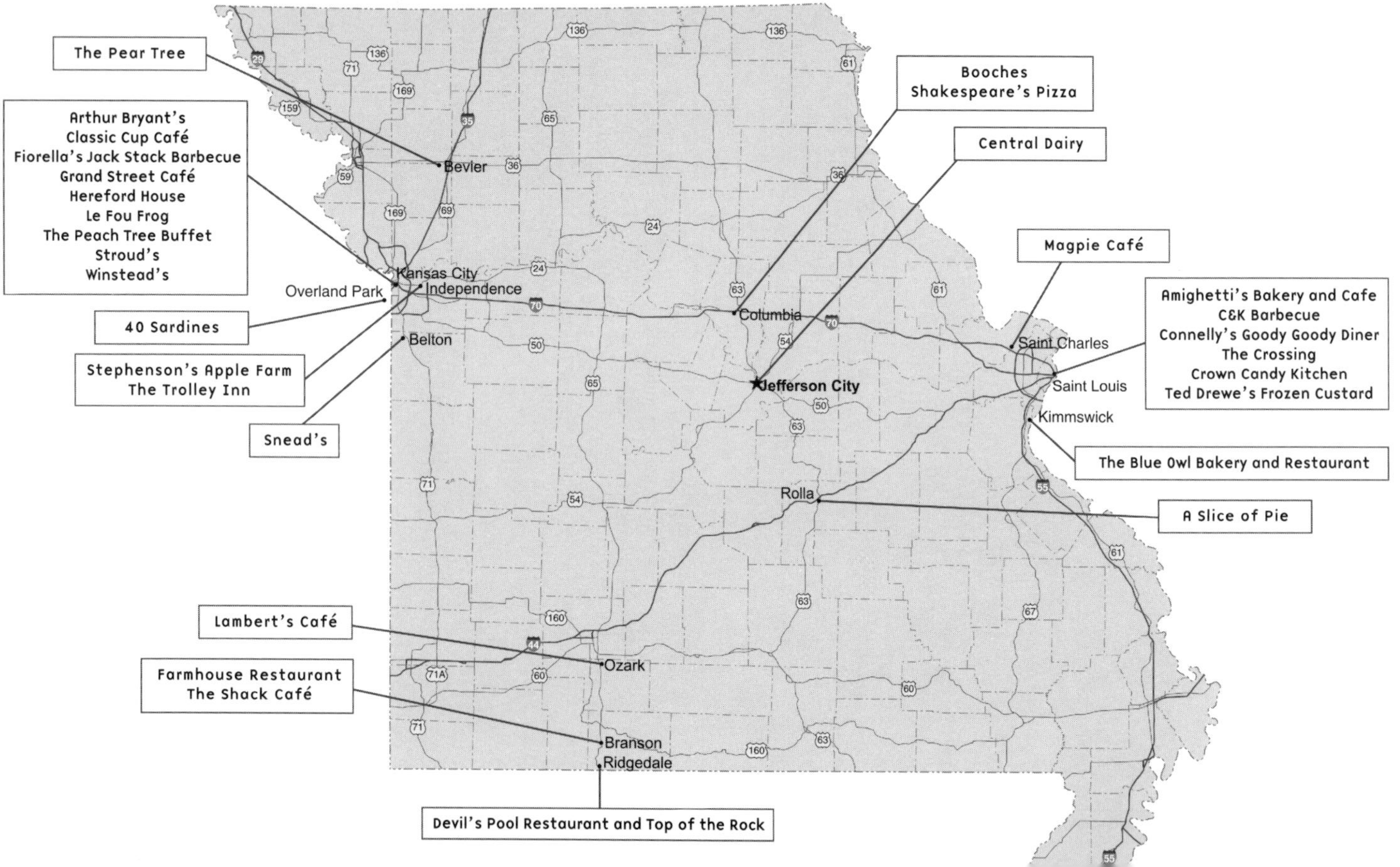

The Pear Tree
Arthur Bryant's
Classic Cup Café
Fiorella's Jack Stack Barbecue
Grand Street Café
Hereford House
Le Fou Frog
The Peach Tree Buffet
Stroud's
Winstead's
40 Sardines
Stephenson's Apple Farm
The Trolley Inn
Snead's
Lambert's Café
Farmhouse Restaurant
The Shack Café
Devil's Pool Restaurant and Top of the Rock
Booches
Shakespeare's Pizza
Central Dairy
Magpie Café
Amighetti's Bakery and Cafe
C&K Barbecue
Connelly's Goody Goody Diner
The Crossing
Crown Candy Kitchen
Ted Drewe's Frozen Custard
The Blue Owl Bakery and Restaurant
A Slice of Pie
Bevier
Kansas City
Overland Park
Independence
Belton
Columbia
Jefferson City
Saint Charles
Saint Louis
Kimmswick
Rolla
Ozark
Branson
Ridgedale

M I S S O U R I

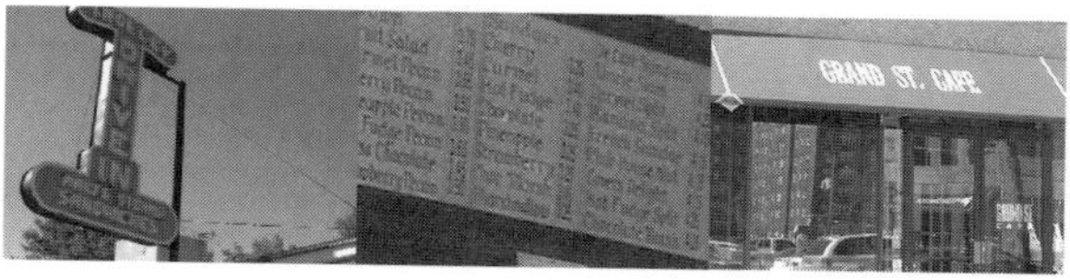

Missouri has as much beautiful food as it does countryside. The state's seventy thousand square miles are defined by the Ozark mountains to the south, the Mississippi river to the east, and rolling hills in the center. The state's two largest cities, St. Louis and Kansas City, have about one-fifth of the population and feel cosmopolitan yet friendly; it's in these cities you find the most extraordinary cuisine.

St. Louis offers Italian food that rivals the old country. On the Hill, Amaghetti's Bakery serves homemade pastas and authentic deli meats. Gian-Tony's (314.772.4893) is famous for its eggplant parmesan and Venetian risotto as well as its cozy, tavern-like setting. In Kansas City, Lidia and Joseph Bastianich opened Lidia's Kansas City (816.221.3722) in a railroad house near the city's historic Union Station. Here you'll find expert pastas made daily plus classics like seared calf's liver with caramelized onions served over creamy, soft polenta.

The university town of Columbia, Missouri, is a nice place to stop if you're traveling. Here you'll find college classics like perfect hamburgers grilled with no fuss on a griddle. I'm thinking of the Booch burger, served in Booches pool hall. Shakespeare's Pizza is another Columbia tradition. Made with the best ingredients Shakespeare's staff can get their hands on, this pizza is the best money can buy. If you want to go upscale in Columbia, try Trattoria Strada Nova (573.442.8992), a stylish bistro in the center of town.

Kansas City is full of culinary gems—from barbecue to steaks, fried chicken and surly French bistros. Stroud's is here; famous for their fried chicken, you'd be wise to try their chicken fried steak as well. Arthur Bryant's offers their famous smoked meats with tangy, thick sauce, but Gate's Barbecue (816.531.7522) is giving Arthur Bryant's world-famous smokehouse a run for its money (Gate's has several locations; the number above is for the store on 1325 Cleaver Boulevard).

Of course, when eating one's way across Missouri, the southern area around Branson cannot be ignored. Comfort food is the way of life—fried catfish being the number one entrée—and most likely, it'll be loaded up on an all-you-can-eat smorgasbord.

Northwest

Arthur Bryant's

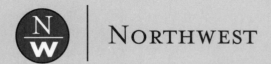

1727 Brooklyn Ave.
Kansas City, Missouri 64127-2530
816.231.1123
www.arthurbryantsbbq.com

Lunch and dinner Monday–Thursday 10 am–9:30 pm, Friday and Saturday 10 am–10 pm, Sunday 11 am–8:30 pm

$11–$18.35

MCC, Beer

Barbecue master Henry Perry and Arthur Bryant's brother, Charlie, ran this popular barbecue joint near the city's municipal baseball stadium in the 1920s. After graduating from college in Texas in 1931, Arthur came to work here with his brother and eventually took over the business in 1940. Bryant moved the restaurant to its current location and worked there until he died of a heart attack, in a bed he kept near the barbecue pit to watch over the flames, in 1982.

Arthur Bryant's is most famous for its pulled barbecue sandwich, piled with approximately twelve ounces of pulled meat on top of a slice of white bread, then topped with several more slices for sopping up Bryant's tangy orange sauce. The meat is smoked slow and low with hickory and oak wood, and the whole thing is wrapped up in butcher paper and hauled over to a table in one of three dining rooms for individual culinary meditation.

Classic Cup Café

301 West 47th St.
Kansas City, Missouri 64112
816.753.1840
www.classiccup.com

Breakfast, lunch, and dinner Monday–Thursday 7 am–10 pm, Friday 7 am–11 pm, Saturday 8 am–11 pm, Sunday 10 am–10 pm; Brunch Sunday 10 am–3:30 pm

Breakfast $4.25–$12; Lunch $7–$13; Dinner first courses $5–$14; Entrees $10–$28

MCC, Full bar

Ann Slegman, restaurant critic for *Kansas City Magazine*, recommended the Classic Cup for breakfast. This sunny café has wrought-iron tables and chairs overlooking the Country Club Plaza, a historic shopping district with cobble-stone streets and tall, white-stucco buildings topped in red-tile roofs. The bookstores, art galleries, and boutique clothiers make this a fun place to stroll after a meal.

Inside the Classic Cup, servers idle past tables with pots full of fresh, gourmet coffee and point out "Daddy's Infamous Waffles" on the menu (the recipe won top honors from *Cooks Illustrated*). Still, the biggest temptation on the menu was bread pudding for breakfast. The pudding is baked in an individual, round soufflé dish and comes to the table sputtering hot. Served drizzled with caramel sauce, this indulgence seems like breakfast fare thanks to fresh fruit crowning the top.

The lunch menu is a "ladies who lunch" classic, including a platter of grilled asparagus, prosciutto, and fresh mozzarella; salads topped with sesame-oat crusted chicken; and herb-roasted salmon. For dinner, you'll find ruby red trout and cracked-pepper Kansas City strip.

Fiorella's Jack Stack Barbecue

13441 Holmes Rd.
Kansas City, Missouri 64145
816.942.9141

www.smokestack.com

Lunch and dinner Monday–Thursday 11 am–10 pm, Friday and Saturday 11 am–10:30 pm, Sunday 11 am–9 pm

Lunch $7–$10; Dinner $7–$36

MCC, Full bar

Along with all the traditional barbecue items, a few stand out to make Jack Stack's unique: Crown prime beef ribs look more like ribs from a dinosaur than ribs from a cow, and you have to be pretty bold to tear into a stack. But of course, barbecue lovers are bold, thus the Crown ribs' bestselling status. Daintier options include the wood-grilled seafood items—jumbo prawns, ruby trout, and salmon.

40 Sardines

11942 Roe Avenue
Overland Park, Kansas 66209
913.451.1040
www.40sardines.com

Lunch Monday–Friday 11 am–2 pm; Dinner Monday–Thursday 5 pm–10 pm, Friday and Saturday 5 pm–11 pm, Sunday 5 pm–9 pm

Lunch first courses $5–$12; Sandwiches and entrees $9–$16; Dinner first courses $5–$15; Entrees $17–$28; Desserts $4–$9

MCC, Full bar

Award-winning chef-owners Debbie Gold and Michael Smith bring fresh, straightforward flavors from around the globe to Kansas City with their local menu built on a foundation of French culinary training. The duo are known for their work with Charlie Trotter's in Chicago and L'Albion in France, but it was their move to the American Restaurant that earned them the most acclaim, garnering the James Beard Award for Best Chefs in the Midwest in 1999.

Gold and Smith set out to make fine dining more affordable with 40 Sardines. The wine list is excellent; twenty-seven demi bottles are offered, including a demi of '99 Opus One for $99, but their budget-wise "20 wines for 20 dollars" gets top-billing on the menu.

On the lunch menu you'll find first courses Belgian endive, watercress, and Asian pear salad, and duck and cabbage egg rolls with plum dipping sauce. The dinner menu usually features the trademark dish, grilled Portuguese sardines with celery, fig, almond, and olive salad. Another favorite is sauteed Campo Lindo chicken livers with lentil salad, frisee, fire-roasted vegetables, and salsa verde.

More adventurous fare includes pan-roasted Broken Arrow Ranch antelope with sweet potato pancetta souffle, dried cherry juice, and spiced pecans. For all the ambition of the menu, Gold and Smith make every effort to keep the tab affordable and maintain a warm, comfortable environment where jackets are not required.

Grand Street Café

4740 Grand Ave.
Kansas City, Missouri 64112

816.561.8000

Lunch and dinner Monday–Thursday 11 am–10 pm, Friday and Saturday 11 am–12 am, Sunday 10:30 am–10 pm; Brunch Sunday

Lunch $7–$13; Dinner first courses $7–$12; Entrees $15–$34

MCC, Full bar

Star chef Michael Peterson might be gone from this contemporary bistro (he's now chef at Kansas City's Segafredo Zanetti), but a rising star has taken his place. Marc Valiani gets nods for a menu filled with seasonal entrees and exciting accompaniments—pine-nut crusted salmon with green apple and onion tart and cranberry-leek relish, and honey-lacquered duck breast with sweet potatoes glistening in ruby port ginger butter and duck-confit rice with currants, almonds, and leeks.

Hereford House

2 E. 20th St.
Kansas City, Missouri 64108
816.842.1080
www.herefordhouse.com

Lunch and dinner Monday–Thursday 11 am–9 pm, Friday 11 am–10 pm; Dinner Saturday 4 pm–10 pm, Sunday 4 pm–9 pm

Lunch $7–$20; Dinner first courses $7–$11; Entrees $13–$35

MCC, Full bar

FYI: Multiple locations

Begun in 1957, Hereford House set up shop near Kansas City's stockyards during the city's heyday as the Midwest's primary beef processor. The restaurant still has much to do with Kansas City's reputation as a great steak destination, with seven cuts of beef in varying sizes (big, bigger, biggest) partnered with hot, fluffy baked potatoes.

Le Fou Frog

400 E. 5th St.
Kansas City, Missouri 64106
816.474.6060

Lunch Wednesday–Friday 11 am–2 pm; Dinner Tuesday–Sunday 5 pm–10 pm

Lunch $5–$15; Dinner entrees $15–$45

MCC, Full bar

French peasant fare such as chartucerie, escargot in puff pastry, and sausage with lentils du puy. You'll find a cozy dining room and an airy terrace for dinner at this bistro, plus a nice wine list. Also on the menu: salted cod with whipped potatoes and garlic croutons, baby spinach salad with roasted beets and gorgonzola dressing, and crispy duck breast with honey lavender sauce.

The Peach Tree Buffet

6800 Eastwood Trafficway
Kansas City, Missouri 64129
816. 923.0099
www.peachtreekansascity.com

Lunch and dinner Sunday–Thursday 11 am–7:30 pm, Friday and Saturday 11 am–8:30 pm

Weekday $9, weekend $10. Special prices for children and seniors.

MCC

Soul food buffet features fried chicken, baked turkey, beef brisket, oven-baked macaroni and cheese, collard greens, black-eyed peas, plus cobblers, cakes, and pudding.

Snead's

1001 E. 71st St.
Belton, Missouri 64012
816.331.9858

Lunch and dinner Wednesday, Thursday, and Sunday 11 am–8 pm, Friday and Saturday 11 am–9 pm. Closed Monday and Tuesday.

Lunch $4.75–$5.70; Dinner $11.35–$17.50

MCC, Beer

Snead's has a large, old brick barbecue pit out back that barbecue lovers from all around come to see. The owner, Bev, says that would-be barbecue restaurateurs model their pits after Snead's, taking measurements and quizzing her on improvements she'd make.

In business since 1956, Snead's draws barbecue fans for its brownies (that's burnt ends), barbecued beans, and log sandwich (a blend of finely chopped smoked meats served on a bun). You'll also find ribs, brisket, and lots of other items on a broad menu.

Stephenson's Apple Farm

16401 E. U.S. Highway 40
Independence, Missouri 64136
☎ 816.373.5400
www.stephensons.bigstep.com

🕘 Lunch Monday–Saturday 11:30 am–4 pm; Dinner Monday–Thursday 4 pm–9 pm, Friday and Saturday 4 pm–10 pm; Sunday brunch 10 am–2 pm; Sunday dinner until 9 pm

$ Lunch $5.50–$14; Dinner first courses $2.25–$6.25; Entrees $13–$24

★ MCC

What started as a fruit stand in 1946 evolved into what is now a much-loved country restaurant surrounded by orchards. As you may expect, the menu lists apple specialties like apple fritters, apple butter, and apple cider. Stephenson's is also famous for its hickory-smoked chicken, ham, ribs, and brisket. The restaurant's recipe for baked chicken, redolent in butter and cream, appeared in an issue of *Better Homes and Gardens*.

Stroud's

1015 E. 85th St.
Kansas City, Missouri 64131-4726
☎ 816.333.2132

🕘 Dinner Monday–Thursday 4 pm–10 pm; Lunch and dinner Friday 11 am–11 pm, Saturday 2 pm–11 pm, Sunday 11 am–10 pm

$ $11–$22

★ MCC, Full bar

! The second location, about eight miles north of downtown Kansas City, is in an old manor house with extensive grounds for kids to play during the inevitable wait for a table. 5410 Northeast Oak Ridge Rd., 816.454.9600

Famous for their iron-skillet fried chicken, Stroud's roadhouse opened in 1933 in an old fireworks stand and was bent on serving more sardines than chicken. When sardines became scarce, the fried chicken rose to fame, earning notoriety with a crispy crust that thinly veils the dense, moist meat within. Mashed potatoes with rich, peppery cream gravy is worth the extra tummy space, too.

Today the roadhouse shows its age with crooked wooden floors, but the friendly service and delicious food make up for it (in fact, they do more than that—there's usually a wait for a table). Aside from the fried chicken, try the fork-tender pork chops, cornmeal-breaded and pan-fried catfish, chicken noodle soup, and crunchy chicken-fried steak topped with cream gravy. Homemade cinnamon rolls and side dishes served family style accompany every meal.

The Trolley Inn

11400 E. Truman Rd.
Independence, Missouri 64050

816.461.9857

Breakfast and lunch Tuesday–Friday 7 am–2 pm, Saturday 7 am–noon

$2.25–$5.50

Cash

This little, old-fashioned trolley car diner serves freshly cut hash browns and hand-formed hamburgers.

Winstead's

1200 Main St.
Kansas City, Missouri 64105

816.221.3339

Breakfast and lunch Monday–Friday 9 am–4 pm

Breakfast $2–$3; Lunch $1.59–$4.85

Cash

Steak burgers are the thing here: thin patties that flop over the sides of a bun that's petite, white, and tender. Winstead's steak burgers come with ketchup, mustard, pickles, and onion, and with that you can get a side of "half and half"—half French fries, half onion rings. Which begs the question, why can't every place be this accommodating? The onion rings are the heavy-battered, crunchy-textured kind, rough on the tongue and slippery sweet inside. Oh, yes, they make an impression.

This is the kind of place where you're seated, and a waitress in a blue and white uniform takes your order and makes change out of her apron at meal's end.

The Pear Tree

208 N. Macon St.
Bevier, Missouri 63532

- ☎ 660.773.6666
- 🕘 Dinner Tuesday–Saturday 4:30 pm–9:30 pm
- $ First courses $5–$12; Entrees $16–$34
- ★ MCC, Full bar
- ! Closed in January

Known for their upscale bistro fare and freshly churned vanilla ice cream with fresh raspberries for dessert.

E | East

Amighetti's Bakery and Cafe

5141 Wilson Ave.
St. Louis, Missouri 63110-3195
314.776.2855
www.amighettis.com

Breakfast and lunch Tuesday–Friday 9 am–7 pm, Saturday 9 am–5:30 pm. Closed Sunday and Monday.

$1.35–$6

MCC, Wine and beer

The bakery opens at 7:30 am and closes earlier than the café. Multiple locations.

This Italian bakery and café is located on "the Hill," a neighborhood known for its Italian restaurants and heritage. The Italian immigrant population soared here in the 1880s until the 1920s, and today seventy-five percent of the population has Italian ancestry. Baseball legends Yogi Berra and Joe Garagiola grew up on the Hill and their childhood homes are across the street from each other.

Amighetti's has limited seating (including a nice courtyard), but a park is nearby with benches and a playground for kids. The most famous item here is the special sub sandwich featuring wonderful, fresh baked bread, Genoa salami, and earthy, Wisconsin brick cheese. But don't count out the pastas: cavatelli with broccoli and spaghetti with garlic butter and fresh mushrooms are also memorable.

The Blue Owl Bakery and Restaurant

6116 Second St.
Kimmswick, Missouri 63053
636.464.3128
www.theblueowl.com

Breakfast and lunch Tuesday–Friday 10 am–3 pm, Saturday and Sunday 10 am–5 pm. Closed Monday.

Breakfast $3.50–$8.50; Lunch $4–$11

MCC

A charming restaurant located on the banks of the Mississippi, the Blue Owl offers a memorable breakfast, lunch, or coffee break. Sweets are the big draw, as Blue Owl's pastries, cookies, and cakes are exceptional: lemon snowflakes, Hungarian butterhorns, and cinnamon nut crescents are just three of many cookies made from scratch daily, plus dozens of pies, cheesecakes, and specialty cakes.

Blue Owl Bakery makes a layer cake related to the Austrian Dobos torte, which features thin layers of sponge cake. Here it's called "dobash" and you'll find five varieties including chocolate Amaretto. Another specialty is the caramel apple pecan pie. With eighteen apples sliced up inside, the pie tops twelve inches in height.

Breakfast and lunch items shouldn't be ignored: four soups are homemade daily including white chili and Canadian cheese, plus lunch plates like meatloaf and chicken and dumplings.

C&K Barbecue

4390 Jennings Station Rd.
St. Louis, Missouri 63121-3329

314.385.8100

Lunch and dinner Monday–Thursday 11 am–11 pm, Friday and Saturday 11 am–1 am, Sunday 11 am–7 pm

$3–$14

MCC

Take out only

C&K is famous for its snoots—pig snouts thinly sliced and cooked until tender, then slathered with sauce. Adventure-averse diners will feel less conflicted with the rib tips, pork steak, or chicken.

Connelly's Goody Goody Diner

5900 Natural Bridge
St. Louis, Missouri 63120
314.383.3333
www.goodygoodydiner.com

Breakfast and lunch Monday–Friday 6 am–2 pm, Saturday 7 am–2 pm. Closed Sunday.

$4–$12

MCC

You can't miss Connelly's Goody Goody Diner. A retro, red sign with flashing neon on the roof grabs your attention and then holds it with a big painting of a ceramic coffee cup. Inside, menu items that make this an unforgetable place include the heart-stopping Wilber omelet and the Hobo breakfast.

The Wilber is a three-egg omelet filled with hash browns, diced green pepper, onion, and tomato, and topped with chili and cheddar cheese. "We thought men would order this more than women when we put it on the menu, but it's the women who get it most of the time!" owner Richard Connelly said. I mocked surprise.

It's hard to turn down the Wilber … until you see the Hobo breakfast bowl: Sausage browned and crisp, cooked up with scrambled eggs, tomatoes, and onions. That's the bottom layer. On top of that, put hash browns, then sausage gravy, then cheddar cheese.

The Crossing

7823 Forsyth Blvd.
St. Louis, Missouri 63105
314.721.7375

Lunch Tuesday–Friday 11:30 am–1:30 pm; Dinner Monday–Thursday 5 pm–9 pm, Friday and Saturday 5 pm–10 pm

Dinner entrees $18–$32

MCC, Full bar

This upscale restaurant got its name from two talented chefs, Jim Fiala and Cary McDowell, with distinct culinary specialties, Italian and French respectively. The restaurant's culinary influences thus crossed paths, but the chefs have now gone their separate ways. Fiala now packs the menu with exciting dishes like smoked salmon salad with fennel, lemon, and capers, and swordfish partnered with fingerling potatoes and chunks of foie gras.

Crown Candy Kitchen

1401 St. Louis Ave.
St. Louis, Missouri 63106-3920

☎ 314.621.9650

🕘 Lunch and dinner Monday–Thursday 10:30 am–9 pm, Friday and Saturday 10:30 am–10 pm, Sunday 12 pm–6 pm

$ Sandwiches $4–$5.25; Malts $3.50

★ MCC

St. Louis is a majestic city filled with beautiful old architecture and in some neighborhoods, the aging buildings have been abandoned. Such is the case in North St. Louis, home to Crown Candy Kitchen. An ice cream parlor established in 1913 with a polished old-fashioned soda fountain and high tin ceilings, Crown Candy Kitchen still manufactures its ice creams in the basement. Thankfully, second-generation owner George Karandzieff refused to move his famous sweet shop. Instead of going to a "better" neighborhood, Karandzieff bettered the neighborhood himself. With the help of his three sons, who now run the restaurant, Crown Candy Kitchen staff mow the lawns of nearby abandoned homes and plant trees.

Kansas City restaurant critic Julie Fallia Earhart met me at Crown Candy Kitchen for lunch and quickly ordered a bacon, lettuce, and tomato sandwich. Clearly, she knows her beat. At Crown Candy Kitchen, they approach the BLT with unmitigated audacity. There is, by Julie's estimate, a quarter-pound of bacon on every single sandwich. Justifiably, Crown cooks go light on the lettuce and tomato—toast can only take so much.

Don't let all that fried bacon keep you from dessert. Ozark black walnut ice cream is not to be missed, nor is the chocolate-banana malt. A house policy standing since 1913 says if you can drink five malts in thirty minutes, all five are free. Don't scoff—fifteen people have done it since 1991.

Magpie Café

903 S. Main St.
St. Charles, Missouri 63301
636.947.3883
Lunch Sunday–Thursday 11 am–3 pm; Lunch and dinner Friday–Saturday 11 am–9 pm
$5–$10
MCC

Magpie Café is a quaint little spot to have lunch in historic St. Charles, home of Missouri's first state capitol. The menu features homemade soups and breads, plus salads and sweets.

Ted Drewe's Frozen Custard

6726 Chippewa St.
St. Louis, Missouri 63109
314.481.2652
www.teddrewes.com
Seven days a week 11 am–11 pm
$1.80–$3.90
MCC

This small, no-frills ice cream stand off of Route 66 is something of a mecca for food lovers. Ted Drewe's Frozen Custard specializes in concretes—a blend of frozen custard and whatever you'd like in it, such as fresh fruit, pistachios, pralines, etc. These are handed to you upside down, held through the window by a spoon handle and straw, a presentation that makes the point: this is real, thick frozen custard made with plenty of cream, sugar, and eggs.

Southeast

A Slice of Pie

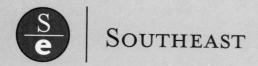

601 Kingshighway
Rolla, Missouri 65401
573.364.6203

Lunch and dinner seven days a week 10 am–10 pm

$3.25–$6

Cash

The people at A Slice of Pie are very friendly and solicitous, and perhaps it is in their nature never to let anyone down. Never, for example, to lack for a certain kind of pie someone might be wanting at any given time. Which may be why the people at A Slice of Pie bake forty to fifty pies a day.

If you ask them what kind of pies they bake, be prepared to sit back and listen: "French silk pie, country custard pie—that's a yellow-custard pie with cream and butter and eggs—peanut butter chocolate swirl pie, apple walnut cake—well I guess that's not a pie. We bake cheesecakes, too. Bailey's Irish Cream cheesecake is the bestseller of those. Boston Cream pie, Tahitian cream pie, we make pot pies like chicken and mushroom pot pie. Coconut meringue is our tallest pie."

You can get your pie as a whole order (that's a big slice) or a half order, depending perhaps on whether you decide to have some quiche (bacon quiche, spinach quiche, salmon quiche) and maybe some homemade soup, of which there are thankfully only two to three a day—"We make all our soups from scratch. We make everything from scratch. Potato soup, bacon soup, chicken noodle soup. And we have salads …"

Southwest

Devil's Pool Restaurant and Top of the Rock

Big Cedar Lodge
612 Devil's Pool Rd.
Ridgedale, Missouri 65739
417.335.5141
www.big-cedar.com

Devil's Pool: Breakfast 7 am–11 am; Lunch 11 am–2 pm; Dinner 5 pm–9:30 pm Seven days a week. Sunday brunch 10 am–2 pm; Top of the Rock: Seven days a week 11 am–9:30 pm

Devil's Pool: First courses $5–$10; Entrees $14–$29; Top of the Rock: First courses $3–$10; Entrees $8–$28

MCC, Full bar

Top of the Rock is located a mile up the road from the lodge. Call for directions.

These two restaurants are located in the Big Cedar Lodge resort overlooking Table Rock Lake, ten miles outside of Branson. Top of the Rock Restaurant specializes in homemade pastas and wood-fired pizza. Menus change with the seasons, with items like pasta with prosciutto, mushroom, and spring pea with parmesan cheese sauce (Italians know it as alla carbonara) showing up in the warmer months and hearty dishes of wild game in the winter. Top of the Rock also has a nice selection of microbrews.

Devil's Pool Restaurant features first courses like smoked Ozark trout served with horseradish cream and lavash bread and entrees like wild mushroom meatloaf. Of course, as is the case almost everywhere in Missouri, you can find dry-aged Kansas City strip on the menu.

Farmhouse Restaurant

119 W. Main St.
Branson, Missouri 65616
417.334.9701

Breakfast, lunch, and dinner seven days a week 7 am–9 pm

$4–$12

MCC

A local favorite for thirty years, the tiny Farmhouse Restaurant is famous for comfort food classics like apple dumplings, country-fried steak, fried catfish, and blackberry cobbler.

Lambert's Café

1800 West State Highway J
(US 65 & Country Rd. J)
Ozark, Missouri 65721
417.581.7655
www.throwedrolls.com

Lunch and dinner Monday–Saturday 10:30 am–9 pm, Sunday 10 am–9 pm

$8–$17

Cash

Multiple locations

Lambert's Café is famous for their throwed rolls. This may sound exotic, as if the way the dough is risen or kneaded adds a light texture or unique character. Au contraire! Lambert's rolls are "throwed" because the staff throw them to you, instead of, say, the more traditional bread basket.

This is ground zero of American comfort food. American, because a restaurant like this becomes famous for the oddest things—We're not talking Appellation D'Origine Controlee. We're talking throwed rolls here. And comfort food, because the home-made freshly baked rolls transport pads of sweet-cream butter.

Also on the menu and not to be ignored are the fried okra, black-eyed peas, fried apples, and chicken fried steak. Notice the operative word, "fried," which is a culinary format entirely justified by a single bite of the crispy brown skillet-fried potatoes and onions.

The Shack Café

108 S. Commercial St.
Branson, Missouri 65616
417.334.3490

Breakfast, lunch, and dinner Monday–Friday 7 am–9 pm, Saturday and Sunday 8 am–7 pm

$4–$7.50

Cash

This classic diner is as famous for its staff as its food: waitresses in crisp uniforms scurry around a grouchy, spatula-wielding cook in white shirt sleeves. Bestsellers include gooseberry cobbler and raisin cream pie.

C | Central

Booches

110 S. 9th St.
Columbia, Missouri 65201-4816
573.874.9519
Monday–Saturday 10 am–midnight
Burgers $2.25
Cash, Full bar

Located near the heart of Missouri University, this is an old pool hall several green, felt-lined tables deep. A griddle sits near the front window, where they fry Booch burgers and serve them up to customers seated on wobbly stools at the bar.

Burgers are one of the only items on the otherwise unimpressive menu, but Booch burgers are important members of the canon of the American burger and thus serve as a role model for all other purveyors of ground beef patties. Not overly messed with, the beauty lies in the burger's simplicity: irregularly formed, half-inch thick—just big enough to make you want more—on a soft, meltaway bun, with ketchup, mustard, pickle, and onions.

Central Dairy

610 Madison St.
Jefferson City, Missouri 65101-3130
573.635.6148
Monday–Saturday 8 am–6 pm, Sunday 10 am–6 pm
$1–$4.50
Cash

This seems to be one of the favorite stop-off points for a treat in Missouri and it's no surprise, what with sundae combinations like the Rock 'n Roll: Eight scoops of Central Dairy's "Missouri milk" ice cream served up in a boat with a spoon or two. Popular flavors made on the premises are Motherlode (vanilla ice cream with a chocolate fudge ribbon and butter brickle nuggets), Moose Tracks, and Bear Claw.

Shakespeare's Pizza

225 S. 9th St.
Columbia, Missouri 65201
☎ 573.449.2454
www.shakespeares.com

🕘 Lunch and dinner seven days a week 11 am–close

$ $6.20–$23.75

★ MCC, Full bar

! Second location—3304 Broadway Business Park Court, 573.447.1202

Shakepeare's Pizza's reputation reverberates across the Midwest. This is in part because of their funny, quirky college-town style and in part due to the ingredients used on their pizzas.

The pizza philosophy at Shakespeare's is use the best, freshest ingredients. Well, obviously, this motto was stolen and made bogus by various national chains. But instead of being mad about that, witness the influence of this funny little place on the big boys.

For Shakespeare's fresh ingredients are more than a lot of blather—it's a modus operandi. Dough is made from scratch daily, and sauce is made from whole tomatoes. Pizza toppings include aged provolone cheese, pepperoni sliced from sticks instead of pre-sliced ("it's too thin!"), and thick, hand-cut mushrooms ("ditto!"). The Italian sausage on Shakespeare's pizzas comes from Italian specialty producers in St. Louis's famous Hill district. Plus, this is just a fun place to hang out.

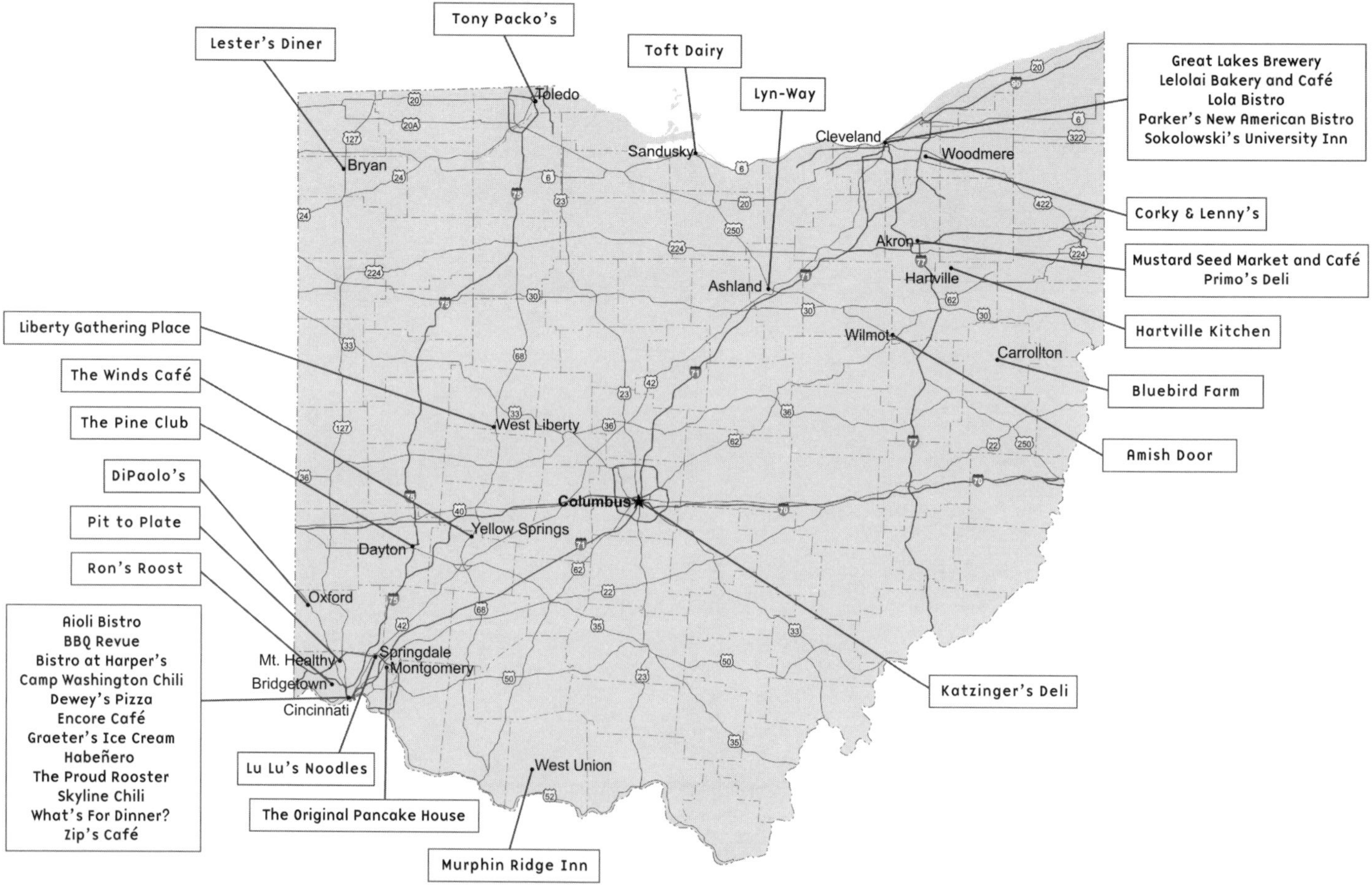
Lester's Diner
Tony Packo's
Toft Dairy
Lyn-Way
Great Lakes Brewery
Lelolai Bakery and Café
Lola Bistro
Parker's New American Bistro
Sokolowski's University Inn
Corky & Lenny's
Mustard Seed Market and Café
Primo's Deli
Hartville Kitchen
Bluebird Farm
Amish Door
Katzinger's Deli
Liberty Gathering Place
The Winds Café
The Pine Club
DiPaolo's
Pit to Plate
Ron's Roost
Aioli Bistro
BBQ Revue
Bistro at Harper's
Camp Washington Chili
Dewey's Pizza
Encore Café
Graeter's Ice Cream
Habeñero
The Proud Rooster
Skyline Chili
What's For Dinner?
Zip's Café
Lu Lu's Noodles
The Original Pancake House
Murphin Ridge Inn
Toledo
Bryan
Sandusky
Cleveland
Woodmere
Akron
Hartville
Ashland
Wilmot
Carrollton
West Liberty
Columbus
Yellow Springs
Dayton
Oxford
Mt. Healthy
Springdale
Montgomery
Bridgetown
Cincinnati
West Union

OHIO

The Amish have strong pull in central Ohio. This is where you find "classics" like the Apple Pie in a Bag. In the off chance that you are an apple-pie-in-a-bag virgin, the dish consists of all the ingredients of an apple pie tossed together in a paper bag and stuffed in the oven. One hour at 350 degrees and voilà! Pastry, Ohio style. There's a crust, and apples, as separate entities, but mixed up like cobbler and handed over with a couple of forks. Makes for good eating in a horse-drawn buggy.

In the southwest of Ohio near Cincinnati, where I'm from, a preponderance of Europeans including Serbians and Greeks migrated to the area and, through an odd melting pot phenomenon, gave birth to Cincinnati-style chili—a spicy hot, thin brown meat-based sauce poured over spaghetti and mounded with finely shredded cheese. It's difficult to convey the dish's many merits to those who haven't tried it; Cincinnati-style chili is absolutely addictive. We also have a strong German heritage in Cincinnati, and you'll find great sausages and hot slaw here. For sausage, try Hofbrauhaus (859.491.7200) across the river in Kentucky. (More details are listed in the Kentucky chapter.) For hot slaw, visit Ron's Roost. If you're looking for French comfort food, try JeanRo downtown (513.621.1465).

Small towns in Ohio are dotted with bed and breakfasts and bistros. In my hometown of Oxford, Alexander House (513.523.1200) uses locally grown produce from area farmers to bring out the best of the season. Murphin Ridge Inn is Ohio's answer to exclusive retreats like Tennessee's Blackberry Farm. Meals prepared by talented chef Richard Cicic are carnally satisfying, like the Black Angus strip steak with balsamic onions and blue cheese butter.

Cleveland has no end to ethnic dining including excellent, full-service Kosher delis and wonderful Italian restaurants serving desserts like tiramisu. According to restaurant critic Laura Taxel, author of *Cleveland Ethnic Eats*, Cleveland has more than 350 authentic ethnic restaurants worth visiting. I can't list them all here (though she does in her book), but I've picked out a few of the best for you.

NW | Northwest

Lester's Diner

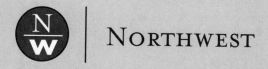

233 South Main St.
Bryan, Ohio 43506
☎ 419.636.1818

Breakfast, lunch, and dinner seven days a week 6 am–10 pm

Breakfast $2–$4; Lunch $4–$6; Dinner specials $4–$6

MCC

Breakfast served all day

A stainless steel diner offering "hard hat specials" in the wee hours of the morning, Lester's is rumored to be the inspiration for Mel's Diner in the TV sitcom *Alice*.

Toft Dairy

3717 Venice Rd.
Sandusky, Ohio 44870
☎ 419.625.5490
www.toftdairy.com

Open daily 8 am–11 pm June–August, 8 am–9 pm September–May

Single cone $1.50; Banana boat $4.50

Cash

Toft's is hard to find—you should probably call to get directions once you hit Sandusky—but even if you get lost, this ice cream is worth every wrong turn. Toft's makes its ice cream in a factory next door to the ice cream parlor's long, white rectangular building. A green stretch of lawn out front is large enough for dozens of kids to play while parents chat into the twilight.

A small tin roof sundae at Toft's could feed three people, but sharing isn't recommended, because the vanilla ice cream is creamy, fresh, and rich, the chocolate sauce is dark and slightly bitter, and Toft's staff take sinful pleasure in squirting as many as six long squirts of chocolate sauce onto the sundae before spooning on as many Spanish peanuts as can fit. The tin roof sundae is cold, sweet, creamy, salty, chocolaty … and unforgettable.

Tony Packo's

1902 Front St.
Toledo, Ohio 43605
419.691.6054
www.tonypackos.com

Lunch and dinner Monday–Thursday 11 am–10 pm, Friday and Saturday 11 am–11 pm, Sunday noon–9 pm

$4.50–$7.50

MCC

Multiple locations

Founded in 1932, Tony Packo's long success is due in part to an early customer's suggestion—put half a sausage on a bun, cover it with meat sauce, and sell it for a nickel. The price, half that of a whole sausage sandwich, was a hit with cash-strapped diners during the Depression and before long the restaurant was a permanent figure in Toledo's Hungarian neighborhood. You'll find plenty of Hungarian specialties, too: chicken Paprikash, stuffed cabbage, and strudels. Check out the displays of hotdog buns signed by celebrities.

Northeast

Amish Door

1210 Winesburg St., US 62
Wilmot, OH 44689
330.359.5464
www.amishdoor.com

Breakfast, lunch, and dinner Monday–Saturday 7 am–8 pm. Fridays and Saturdays in the summer 7 am–9 pm. Closed Sunday.

Sandwiches $2.79–$4.29; Entrees $5.49–$10.79; All-you-can-eat family style dinners $11.79–$13.29

MCC

Amish Door sells apple pie in a bag on Saturdays. Entrees include broasted chicken, roast pork, and country ham.

Bluebird Farm

190 Alamo Rd.
Carrollton, Ohio 44615-9581
330.627.7980

Lunch Tuesday–Sunday 11 am–4 pm; Dinner Friday and Saturday 4 pm–8 pm. Closed January through March.

Lunch $5.75–$7; Dinner $10–$16

Cash

This historic farmhouse built by early Ohio settlers has three floors for dining, and each is decorated differently. Since this used to be a house, each bathroom still has a bathtub, and in one bathtub there's a life-size gorilla in a "bubble bath" of glass globes. Bluebird Farm has a quarter-mile garden path for walking after a meal, plus a gift shop and a toy museum with special displays of historic American dolls like Raggedy Ann and Andy and German Steiff stuffed animals.

Corky & Lenny's

27091 Chagrin Blvd.
Woodmere, Ohio 44122
216.464.3838
www.corkyandlennys.com

Breakfast, lunch, and dinner Sunday–Friday 7 am–11 pm, Saturday 7 am–midnight

Breakfast $1.65–$8.10; Soups, sandwiches, and salads $3–$11.25; Entrees $7.50–$18.50

MCC, Wine

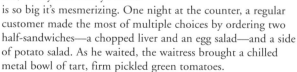

Corky and Lenny's is tucked in a strip mall in suburban Akron, and you'll do right to dine here breakfast through dinner. At the front of the deep, good-looking restaurant is a deli loaded with wonderful desserts, including little pastries called rugalach, and traditional take-out items like pickled herring, smoked whitefish, meat, potato or corned beef knishes, and homemade soups sold by the pint or quart.

In true Jewish deli fashion, Corky and Lenny's menu is so big it's mesmerizing. One night at the counter, a regular customer made the most of multiple choices by ordering two half-sandwiches—a chopped liver and an egg salad—and a side of potato salad. As he waited, the waitress brought a chilled metal bowl of tart, firm pickled green tomatoes.

The corned beef at Corky and Lenny's is lean and zesty, sliced thin and piled high. But it would be alone in the world without the bread on which it rests: yeasty and warm, this bread holds the meat like a mother holds her child. Small covered bowls of fresh horseradish add the right accompaniment.

Great Lakes Brewery

2516 Market Ave.
Cleveland, Ohio 44113
216.771.4404
www.greatlakesbrewing.com

Lunch and dinner Monday–Thursday 11:30 am–midnight, Friday and Saturday 11:30 am–1:00 am. Closed Sunday.

Starters, soups, and salads $5–$11; Entrees $8–$20; Desserts $3.75–$6

MCC, Full bar

Just a stone's throw from Cleveland's famous West Side Market, Great Lakes Brewery is a micro-brewery, bottling and selling nine specialty brews in Ohio, Michigan, Pennsylvania, and Kentucky. Visit the brewery not just for these award-winning brews but also for the food: walleye pike from Lake Erie is prominent on the menu as is traditional pub fare like a sausage sampler plate with Louisiana hot sausages and sautéed peppers and onions. The menu features trendier fare, too: coffee and peppercorn-crusted filet of beef finished with a merlot reduction, and apple- and ginger-spiked crab cakes over wilted mesclun greens. For dessert, try bread pudding with whiskey caramel sauce.

The brewery offers facility tours showcasing founders Patrick and Dan Conway's environmental policy for zero waste. Spent hops and grain from making beer are used to grow the restaurant's organic mushrooms and are also an ingredient in house-made pretzels. Great Lakes gives the remaining spent grain to local farmers who use it for animal feed and to grow pesticide-free produce. These farmers sell their top-shelf ingredients to Great Lakes Brewery.

The restaurant is in a turn-of-the-century Victorian building steeped in local flavor. Elliot Ness, the crime-fighting chief of police in Cleveland, spent time at the building when it was a bar in the 1940s and bullet holes still pockmark the woodwork. Great Lakes Brewery basks in Cleveland history, and named its best-selling pale ale "Burning River" for when the Cuyahoga caught fire in 1969.

Hartville Kitchen

1015 Edison St. NW
Hartville, Ohio 44632
330.877.9353
www.hartvillekitchen.com

Monday, Tuesday, Thursday–Saturday 11 am–8 pm. Closed Wednesday and Sunday.

Soups, salads and sandwiches $1.80–$7; Entrees $8.50–$9.25; Desserts $1.85–$8.50 (whole pie)

MCC

The market is open year round Monday and Thursday, 8 am–4 pm, and Saturday 8 am–5 pm. For more information call 330.877.9860.

I feel the need to prepare you. Hartville Kitchen is not a restaurant; it is a macrocosm. The original Hartville Kitchen was founded in 1966 in a humble wooden barn with an open air market selling Amish quilts next door. People as far as three states away loved Hartville Kitchen so much that the place literally fell down. So the owners, the Miller family, built a new one.

Clearly the Millers don't believe in doing anything halfway: the new Hartville Kitchen is eighty-four thousand square feet and can seat more than four hundred people plus banquet rooms. That's just the restaurant building. Beyond the dizzying expanse of twenty acres of parking lot you'll find the Hartville Market, which features a two-story indoor section with almost two hundred vendors and one hundred thousand square feet of shops. The outdoor section of the market houses one thousand more vendors selling Amish meats and cheeses, crafts, and furniture.

The restaurant serves "homestyle" cooking. When a restaurant substitutes "style" for "made," it usually means there are a few cans opening in the kitchen, but the food still has an authentic ring. Dishes to try include the roast pork sandwich with mashed potatoes and gravy, fried chicken, and breaded pork chops. Saimi Bergmann, restaurant critic and food writer for the *Canton Repository*, introduced me to Hartville Kitchen, and together we sampled rhubarb crumb pie and gave it a starred review.

Lelolai Bakery and Café

1889 W. 25th St.
Cleveland, Ohio 44113
216.771.9956

Breakfast and lunch Monday–Wednesday 7:45 am–5 pm, Thursday–Saturday 7:45 am–6 pm. Closed Sunday.

$.75–$5.50

MCC

This casual ethnic spot is a nice stop for Puerto Rican coffee and pastelillos, small puff pastries dusted with powdered sugar. Try the quesitos, guava and cheese filled pastries, and freshly made coconut flan. If you're a fan of the Cuban sandwich, try it here: roasted pork, ham, cheese, and tomato are loaded onto Creole-style bread and toasted in a sandwich press to make a hot, crunchy, addictive street food.

Lola Bistro

900 Literary Rd.
Cleveland, Ohio 44113
216.771.5652
www.lolabistro.com

Dinner Tuesday–Thursday 5 pm–midnight, Friday and Saturday 5 pm–1 am, Sunday 5 pm–11 pm

First courses $6–$9; Entrees $19–$26

MCC, Full bar

Reservations accepted

Chef Michael Symon uses locally grown ingredients to create buzz-worthy dishes like pan-fried walleye over a bed of diced potatoes, bacon, and peas. Halibut is brightened with pickled onions and citrus butter. A plate of pecan-crusted chicken is a caricature of comfort food, partnered with creamy, just-picked corn and carrot puree.

Lyn-Way

1320 Cleveland Ave.
Ashland, Ohio 44805

419.281.8911

Breakfast, lunch, and dinner Monday–Thursday 6 am–10 pm, Friday and Saturday 6 am–11 pm; Dinner Sunday 5 pm–10 pm

Breakfast $1.49–$5.59; Soups, salads, and sandwiches $1.89–$6; Entrees $5.29–$9.59

MCC

Lyn-Way is a friendly neighborhood restaurant in a white, unassuming building on the edge of town, next to a small golf course. A sign posted near the door says "Serving Ashland Since 1951" and "Please remove cleats before entering." Coffee is constantly brewing on the industrial-size Bunn behind the counter, and breakfast is served until eleven o' clock. Waitresses wear white aprons and embrace their job with gusto, serving fried mush that's hot and crispy on the outside, dense and moist inside, served with a pad of butter sealed in plastic. Lunch could be an open-faced roast beef or hot shredded chicken sandwich with mashed potatoes and chicken gravy. For dessert, a three-dip banana split is $3.69, made with Smith's ice cream from nearby Orrville, Ohio.

Mustard Seed Market and Café

3885 W. Market St.
Akron, Ohio 44333-2449
330.666.7333
www.mustardseedmarket.com

Lunch and dinner Monday–Thursday 11 am–8 pm, Friday and Saturday 11 am–9 pm; Brunch Sunday 10:30 am–2:30 pm

Salads and sandwiches $3–$12; Entrees $6–$24

MCC, Wine and beer

This is a café in an upscale natural foods market, but it's better than that. Mustard Seed Café is warm and cozy: The café is in the back of the store on the second floor, and once you ascend the steps you feel nicely separated—no more fluorescent lights, no more loud speakers. It's carpeted and somewhat dark. A hostess seats you at unclothed Corian-surfaced tables, or you can sit at the juice and wine bar where Mustard Seed Market sells a nice variety of wines by the glass.

Arrive early for the affordable early bird "café dinner" menu, featuring Southwest poblano chile shrimp, a plateful of warmly spiced plump shrimp atop a bed of mesclun greens, and a veggie quesadilla stuffed to the edges with peppers, onions, tomatoes, and lots more veggies, plus jack and cheddar cheese.

Mustard Seed Market features organic produce, free-range animal products, and whole foods, and that's what you'll find in the café: lots of vegetarian and vegan fare. But a carnivore has choices too. Bison Delmonico is a ribeye dusted with Cajun spices, grilled and served with marinated roasted vegetables. An added bonus: this is a kid-friendly place—parents can enjoy a guilt-free meal because of the casual grocery store setting.

Parker's New American Bistro

2801 Bridge Ave.
Cleveland, Ohio 44113-3013
216.771.7130

Dinner Monday–Thursday 5 pm–10 pm, Friday and Saturday 5 pm–11 pm. Closed Sunday.

First courses $4–$9; Entrees $16–$29

MCC, Full bar

Chef/owner Parker Bosley preaches the benefits of locally grown, seasonal produce and makes a compelling case for their use in his kitchen. Dishes like roasted beets in orange-sherry vinaigrette and country pork terrine communicate beyond words. Parker's menu changes regularly, but look for dishes like slow-roasted pork loin with Ohio farmers' rhubarb sauce, Killbuck Valley mushroom risotto, and sweetbreads with port wine reduction.

Primo's Deli

1707 Wooster Pike
Akron, Ohio 44320
330.745.9056

Lunch and dinner Monday–Saturday 10 am–8 pm. Closed Sunday.

Sandwiches $3.79–$8.59

MCC, Beer

Primo's Deli is well-known for two things: Hot Italian subs and a great selection of micro-brews. The selection of more than two hundred brands of bottled beer includes Bell's, Victory, Orval, Stone, Great Lakes, DuPont, and Fantome Saisson.

Sokolowski's University Inn

1201 University Rd.
Cleveland, Ohio 44113
216.771.9236
www.sokolowskis.com

Lunch Monday–Friday 11 am–3 pm; Dinner Friday 5 pm–9 pm, Saturday 4 pm–9 pm

Lunch $5.75–$8; Dinner $8.75–$16

MCC, Full bar

The question with Sokolowski's neighborhood eatery is this: What has more charm, the people or the food? As you grab a tray and make your way down the cafeteria line, look up from your Salisbury steak to check out the framed potraits of the Sokolowski family with the former president of Poland, Lech Walesa, and polka legend Eddie Blazowczyk. Bestselling lunch and dinner items are the sauteed pierogies with onions and butter, beer-battered lake fish, and smoked kielbasa.

SOUTHWEST

AIOLI BISTRO

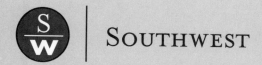

700 Elm St.
Cincinnati, Ohio 45202
513.929.0525
www.aiolibistro.com

Lunch Monday–Friday 11:30 am–2 pm; Dinner Monday–Thursday 5:30 pm–9:30 pm, Friday and Saturday 5:30 pm–10 pm

Lunch $5–$11.50; Dinner starters $5–$10; Entrees $15–$25

MCC, Full bar

Chef/owner Julie Francis's warm, vibrant restaurant is in conversation with the Midwest's best contemporary bistros. The menu changes regularly and is filled with local ingredients. A first course of salmon tartare with truffled celery root and apple slaw, marinated baby beets, and salmon roe is smooth and rosy and fragrant with truffle oil. Paper-thin layers of ravioli veil wild mushrooms, butternut squash, and braised escarole on a bath of rosemary-infused Marsala cream.

Francis's years in New Mexico still form part of her culinary consciousness. Chiles have a prominent place on her menu in dishes such as a first course of chipotle chile-braised beef with blue corn cakes, guacamole, and red chile sauce, and duck confit tamale with mole rojo and sun-dried cherry chutney. But the menu reflects an even broader creative drive, sprinkled with items like green tea soba noodles, root vegetable dumplings, and spiced carrot flan.

BBQ REVUE

4725 Madison Rd.
Cincinnati, Ohio 45227-1425
513.871.3500

Lunch and dinner Tuesday–Saturday 11 am–8 pm, Sunday noon–8 pm

Full slab $15.95; Half slab $8.25; Sides $1.25 (small) –$2.50 (large)

MCC, Full bar

Ribs are marinated in dry rub for ten hours before being smoked with hickory wood. Macaroni and cheese is gooey and soft, with crusty edges.

Bistro at Harper's

11384 Montgomery Rd.
Cincinnati, Ohio 45249-2313

513.489-9777

Lunch Monday–Friday 11 am–4 pm; Dinner Monday–Thursday 4 pm–9 pm, Friday 4 pm–11 pm, Saturday 5 pm–11 pm, Sunday 5 pm–9 pm.

First courses $6–$9; Sandwiches and burgers $7–$8; Entrees $14–$17; Desserts $6–$7

MCC, Full bar

Bistro at Harper's has all the appeal of a neighborhood grill but kicks up the caliber a notch with creative dishes that don't just taste good—they evoke curiosity. The "flying pig" is a roasted pork tenderloin accompanied by a savory bread pudding of mushrooms and pancetta plus a lovely bundle of verdant spinach. The pork is slow-roasted, tender, and flavorful, but the bread pudding is altogether mystic.

Also on the menu: A standout version of first-course Asian tacos with sweet-salty, stir-fried chicken and crunchy water chestnuts piled high with thin white rice noodles; mussels served with crostini spread with roasted garlic and leeks; and a fine chile-glazed salmon, pan-seared and laid on a bed of teriyaki-sauced udon noodles and accompanied by a stack of Chinese vegetables. Don't skip dessert; try a handmade cone dipped in toffee and pecans, filled with cobbler and homemade ice cream, and topped with a superfluous dollop of whipped cream.

Camp Washington Chili

Colerain Ave. and Hopple St., off Interstate 75
Cincinnati, Ohio 45225-1891

☎ 513.541.0061

🕘 24 hours Monday–Saturday. Closed Sunday.

$ $1.20–$5

★ Cash

Camp Washington Chili is a Cincinnati landmark in a new building. The chili parlor's original home was taken down to make way for an added street lane after a twenty-four-year battle between the city and owner John Johnson. But the spanking new location is spacious and sparkling clean, only a few feet from the original. Plus, the double-deckers, coneys, and three-ways taste the same.

Dewey's Pizza

3014 Madison Rd.
Cincinnati, Ohio 45209-1710

☎ 513.731.7755
www.deweyspizza.com

🕘 Lunch and dinner Monday–Thursday 11 am–10 pm, Friday and Saturday 11 am–11 pm, Sunday 4 pm–10 pm

$ Base pizza price $7–$11; Regular and gourmet ingredients $1–$1.75

★ MCC, Wine and beer

! Multiple locations

Hand-tossed pizzas with gourmet ingredients like prosciutto, pine nuts, and fontina cheese, plus big, bodacious salads.

DiPaolo's

77 S. Main St.
Oxford, Ohio 45056

☎ 513.523.1541

Breakfast seven days a week 7 am–10 am; Lunch Monday–Saturday 11 am–2 pm; Dinner Sunday–Thursday 5 pm–9 pm, Friday and Saturday 5 pm–10 pm; Brunch Sunday 11 am–2 pm

First courses $6–$8; Entrees $16–$27

MCC, Full bar

To the Oxford residents and Miami University students in this red-brick-and-ivy college town, DiPaolo's is the place to toast special occasions. Located in the Elms Hotel near the busy main square, DiPaolo's second floor dining room is lined with arched windows overlooking the small town's picturesque streets. DiPaolo's classics include veal scaloppine in port wine sauce with herbed potato gnocchi, and chicken piccata with artichoke hearts and capers in lemony cream. The menu features a bevy of nightly specials like Virginia soft shell crab meuniere and gulf coast escolar in champagne-tarragon sauce.

Encore Café

7305 Tylers Corner Dr.
West Chester, Ohio 45069-6344
513.759.4624
www.encorecafe.com

Lunch Monday–Friday 11 am–3 pm; Dinner Monday–Friday 4 pm–10 pm, Friday and Saturday 4 pm–11 pm

Lunch pizzas $6–$10; Entrée salads $8–$12; Sandwiches $7–$9; Dinner starters $3.25–$12; Entrees $14–$25; Desserts $6.25

MCC, Full bar

Second location—9521 Fields-Ertel Rd., Loveland, 513.774.7072

Husband and wife chef team Paul and Pam Sturkey must have chef skills in their genes. Such is the seamlessness of the service at Encore and the grace of the menu. Try cedar-planked sea scallops, seafood gumbo, and New Zealand lamb chops with orange-ginger reduction. Pam Sturkey is the pastry chef, and desserts are a must here (the "sundae of all sundaes" is topped with sugared cashews, Bailey's truffles, peanut butter squares, and ginger snaps).

Graeter's Ice Cream

332 Ludlow Ave.
Cincinnati, Ohio 45220-2019
513.281.4749
www.graeters.com

Monday–Saturday 7 am–10:45 pm, Sunday 9 am–10:45 pm

Single $2.50; Double $2.95; Pint $3.95

MCC

Multiple locations

Graeter's ice cream is made in small batches using the "French pot" method: swirling the cream in cold pots so that it's extra dense (most commercial ice creams are whipped with air). Each month, Graeter's has a special flavor, and on the regular menu, must-haves are raspberry chocolate chip, amaretto crunch, and strawberry sorbet.

Habañero

358 Ludlow Ave.
Cincinnati, Ohio 45220-2019
513.961.6800

Lunch and dinner 11 am–11 pm daily

$5–$7

MCC, Wine and beer

Down-to-earth appreciation of the good life characterizes Habañero's Latin-American cuisine. Tiny copper lights dangle above comfy booths where people sit swilling pitchers of sangria and micro-brew beer. The walls and floor wear warm terracotta, gold, and deep blue hues. Brazilian samba plays lightly on the air.

Stand at the counter to order. The menu is posted on the wall and includes plenty of vegetarian options: Chuba cabre combines cinnamon-roasted pumpkin, butternut and acorn squash, and apple and green chile salsa. A house salad is a refreshing tumble of thinly sliced mixed greens, tomatoes, and roasted red peppers tossed with orange-cilantro vinaigrette and loaded into a tortilla bowl.

Latin-American inspired entrees like calypso chicken and arroyo hondo feature chef-worthy compilations of ingredients like a freshly made pineapple-almond salsa (in the case of the chicken) and flat iron steak rubbed with spices and topped with fire-roasted chipotle chile salsa with goat cheese and sautéed onions. These carefully prepared and constructed entrees are then casually wrapped in an oversized tortilla.

Lu Lu's Noodles

135 W. Kemper Rd.
Springdale, Ohio 45246-2511
513.671.4949

Lunch and dinner Monday–Thursday 11 am–9:30 pm, Friday–Saturday 11 am–10 pm

Soups and starters $2–$4; Noodle bowls $4–$6; Chinese entrees $7–$9

Cash

Lu Lu's serves more than fifteen kinds of noodle dishes, including steaming pho, a traditional Vietnamese soup of clear broth and long, thin noodles, and lard nar, pan-fried rice noodles in brown sauce with plenty of crisp veggies. Also worth a try is the stir-fried bean curd with vegetables.

Murphin Ridge Inn

750 Murphin Ridge Rd.
West Union, Ohio 45693
937.544.2263
www.murphinridgeinn.com

Dinner Tuesday–Saturday 5–8 pm

Three-course dinner $20–$27

MCC

Reservations required

Murphin Ridge Inn is a gourmet getaway full of charm, and lucky for us, its four candle-lit dining rooms are open to the public during dinner. Chef Richard Cicic and proprietors Sherry and Darryl McKenney are dedicated to a seasonal menu featuring ingredients from the Murphin Ridge farm. Anticipate entrees like golden crispy grouper and rack of lamb with mint sauce.

The Original Pancake House

9977 Montgomery Rd.
Montgomery, Ohio 45242-5311
☎ 513.745.0555

🕘 Breakfast and lunch Monday–Friday 7 am–2 pm, Saturday and Sunday 7 am–3 pm

$ $3.50–$8.50

★ MCC

The Original Pancake House's nationwide success could be attributed to the glories of their Dutch baby and apple pancakes. But the efforts made to assure each franchise meets a high standard should also get credit. Both attributes contribute to this location's success. Be prepared to wait for a table.

The Pine Club

1926 Brown St.
Dayton, Ohio 45409-2456
☎ 937.228.5371
www.thepineclub.com

🕘 Dinner Monday–Thursday 5 pm–midnight, Friday and Saturday 5 pm–1 am

$ First courses $3–$10; Entrees $16–$30 (double porterhouse is $60)

★ Cash, Full bar

The Pine Club is the kind of restaurant that develops a devoted following despite (or because of) its many quirks. This restaurant takes no reservations, has no non-smoking section, offers no dessert and won't accept credit cards. Yet the fine, aged steaks and dark 1940s supperclub décor make for a memorable meal, and people love it.

Pit to Plate

1527 Compton Rd.
Mt. Healthy, Ohio 45231-3455

513.931.9100

Monday–Thursday 11 am–9 pm, Friday and Saturday 11 am–10 pm

Sandwiches $5–$5.50; Plates with two sides $7–$18

MCC

Owner Dianne Creech has come close to creating barbecue perfection: fall-apart tender pork shoulder, smoky beef brisket, and succulent baby back ribs. Southern-accented sides include tart cucumber and onion salad, green beans with bits of smoked kielbasa, rich mashed potatoes, and mustardy deviled eggs crowned with green, pimento-stuffed olives. Save room for seven-flavor pound cake and creamy sweet chess pie.

A long-time restaurant worker, Ms. Creech got the idea for her restaurant while eating in a Nashville joint. The barbecue impressed her so much, she found out where the smoker was made, ordered one just like it from Dallas, rented a truck, and brought the two-ton, black carbon-steel cooker back to Cincinnati. Those who love real barbecue are thankful she made the trip.

The Proud Rooster

345 Ludlow Ave.
Cincinnati, Ohio

513.281.4965

Breakfast and lunch seven days a week

Breakfast $2–$4; Lunch $4.50–$6

Cash

This is a small, owner-run "greasy spoon" in a charming, somewhat bohemian neighborhood near the University of Cincinnati. If you like fried eggs, home fries with onions, crisp bacon, and bottomless cups of coffee, this is your place. The Proud Rooster also sells great fried chicken at lunch.

Ron's Roost

3853 Race Rd.
Bridgetown, Ohio 45211
513.574.0222

Lunch and dinner Monday–Thursday 11 am–9:30 pm, Friday and Saturday 11 am–10 pm, Sunday 10 am–9 pm

First courses $2.50–$5; Entrees $7–$16

MCC, Full bar

In its forty-year history, Ron's Roost has remodeled and expanded, most recently to accommodate up to 230 guests. But after the construction workers leave and the dust settles, back up go the photographs of Pete Rose on the walls and the big red and white rooster on the roof. Sure, things can change, but only some things.

With a name like Ron's Roost, you'd be right to assume: order the chicken. But this is a place with a strong German heritage, so be sure to try the mock turtle soup and hot slaw with fat back.

Skyline Chili

290 Ludlow Ave.
Cincinnati, Ohio 45220
513.221.2142
www.skyline.com

Lunch and dinner Monday–Friday 10 am–3 am, Friday and Saturday 10 am–4 am, Sunday 11 am–midnight

$1.29–$5.89

MCC

Multiple locations

Cincinnati is famous for its chili, and this is one of the city's best chili parlors. Open until early morning, watching the nightlife unfold here is a treat unto itself—but everything's better with a three-way and a couple of cheese coneys. The menu also includes salads, baked potatoes, and black bean burritos.

What's For Dinner?

3009 O'Bryon St.
Cincinnati, Ohio 452
513.321.4404

Lunch and dinner Monday–Thursday 11 am–9 pm, Friday and Saturday 1 pm–11 pm

First courses $7–$8.50; Entrees $7.50–$19

MCC, Full bar

Homey-but-better-than-homemade takeout food in a sunny, friendly environment makes "What's for Dinner?" worth a stop. The dining room cobbles together mismatched furniture and healthy food. There's a big focus on fresh vegetables, with dishes like vegetarian ratatouille risotto, creamy and speckled with tomato, zucchini, and yellow squash. Try expert seafood dishes like wild striped bass, sweet and firm in a pistachio crust, bundled on top with vibrant vegetables and a three-bean ragout.

The Winds Café

215 Xenia Ave.
Yellow Springs, Ohio 45387
937.767.1144
www.windscafe.com

Lunch and dinner Tuesday–Saturday 11:30 am–2 pm and 5 pm–10 pm; Brunch Sunday 10 am–2 pm

Brunch $6–$15; Lunch $6–$12; Dinner first courses $5–$14; Entrees $19–$24

MCC, Full bar

The Winds' menu is constantly changing, but you can always rely on its gourmet, world-beat bent. A recent brunch menu included browned onion, bacon, and pepper pancakes with grilled salmon and cheddar gravy. For dinner? Braised duck leg with lemon, rum, and figs. A wine cellar next door adds unusual wines to the eclectic mix.

Zip's Café

1036 Delta Ave.
Cincinnati, Ohio 45208-3104
☎ 513.871.9876

Lunch and dinner Monday–Saturday 10:30 am–11 pm, Sunday 11 am–11 pm

Soups and salads $1.25–$6; Sandwiches and burgers $1.75–$5

MCC, Full bar

Zip's Café is a quirky place to eat in a fun area of Cincinnati. Located on Mt. Lookout square, this small, dark café is tucked into the rolling hills just east of downtown, amid affluent Hyde Park and hip, colorful Columbia Tusculum. If you've never been to Cincinnati before, you should reserve some time to explore these neighborhoods before or after your meal.

The café only seats about thirty people; waiting for a seat is standard, but tables turn over quickly as the kitchen and servers move at supersonic speed. An electric train rattles along tracks that run the length of the ceiling above the noise from the dining room and the short wooden bar.

Zipburgers and chili are what you should order here. Don't bother with the rest, other than french fries and cold beer on tap. Zipburgers are crispy on the edges, just a tinge of pink inside, and made of flavorful, fresh beef. Chili is not the native Cincinnati style, but what the rest of the country is used to: red, thick broth stocked with juicy chunks of beef and kidney beans, served with sour cream and shredded cheese.

C | Central

Katzinger's Deli

475 S. 3rd St.
Columbus, Ohio 43215
614.228.3354
www.katzingers.com

Breakfast, lunch, and dinner Monday–Friday 8:30 am–8:30 pm, Saturday and Sunday 9 am–8:30 pm

Sandwiches $5–$10.50; Soups $1.50–$2.25; Salads $5–$9

MCC

Katzinger's is an exceptional deli, with long glass cases filled with fresh, homemade salads, knishes, blintzes, and desserts. The sandwich board boasts almost sixty variations, and aisles are lined with extensive varieties of first-cold-press extra virgin olive oil and aged balsamic vinegar. Just off the I-70/71 interchange in German Village, Katzinger's is an easy road trip stop, though it would be a worthy destination from miles away.

Sandwich number 41 is my favorite: Chicken salad, applewood smoked bacon, Switzerland Swiss, lettuce, tomato, mayonnaise, and honey mustard on rye. The bread has a crunchy and crisp crust that no child would ask his mother to trim, and a fluffy delicate center. Katzinger's chicken salad is mild and finely chopped, a contrast with hearty, thick bacon. Fresh dill and hot pickles await in big wooden barrels by the cash register.

Katzinger's is not cheap—a sandwich with a bottle of water set me back $10—but the cost all goes to ingredients, and it's worth it. The atmosphere is casual deli. Wait at the counter to order, then grab a seat; staff bring your sandwich out to you. If you have time after eating, take a stroll up the street to enjoy the quaintness of German Village. A block away, you'll find Cup-O-Joe coffee shop and a thirty-two-room book shop called the Book Loft.

Liberty Gathering Place

111 North Detroit St.
West Liberty, Ohio 43357

☎ 937.465.3081

🕐 Breakfast, lunch, and dinner Monday–Friday 5:30 am–7:30 pm, Saturday 6 am–7:30 pm, Sunday 8 am–2:30 pm

$ Breakfast $2–$4; Lunch $2.25–$5; Dinner $6–$8

★ Cash

Macaroni salad and scalloped corn grab the spotlight here, even among luscious ham loaf and crisp pork tenderloin sandwiches.

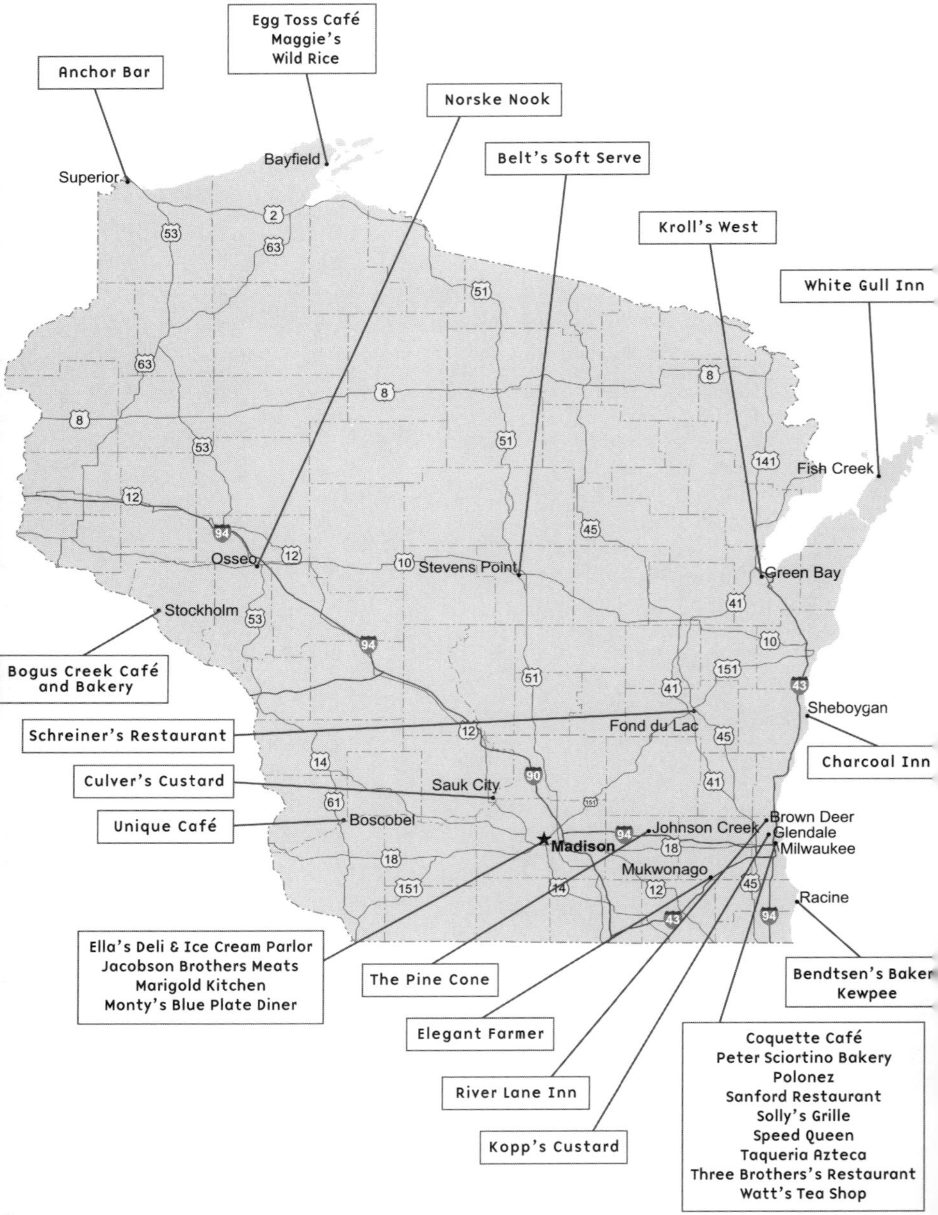
Egg Toss Café
Maggie's
Wild Rice
Anchor Bar
Norske Nook
Belt's Soft Serve
Kroll's West
White Gull Inn
Bayfield
Superior
Fish Creek
Osseo
Stevens Point
Green Bay
Stockholm
Bogus Creek Café and Bakery
Sheboygan
Schreiner's Restaurant
Fond du Lac
Charcoal Inn
Culver's Custard
Sauk City
Unique Café
Boscobel
Brown Deer
Johnson Creek
Glendale
Madison
Milwaukee
Mukwonago
Racine
Ella's Deli & Ice Cream Parlor
Jacobson Brothers Meats
Marigold Kitchen
Monty's Blue Plate Diner
The Pine Cone
Bendtsen's Baker
Kewpee
Elegant Farmer
River Lane Inn
Kopp's Custard
Coquette Café
Peter Sciortino Bakery
Polonez
Sanford Restaurant
Solly's Grille
Speed Queen
Taqueria Azteca
Three Brothers's Restaurant
Watt's Tea Shop

WISCONSIN

Each Midwestern state has a distinct culinary personality. Wisconsin's is defined in part by its Northern-European roots and its dairy farms. Wonderful fresh farm cheeses are all over menus here, with "Wisconsin" versions of hamburgers and pizzas featuring four or more kinds of Wisconsin cheese piled on top.

The large influx from countries like Poland in the late nineteenth and early twentieth century brought a strong Catholic heritage whose influence is notable in the state-wide phenomenon of Friday night fish fries. From high-style bistros to family-friendly supper clubs, fish fries are a delicious way to spend Friday evenings. Even TGI Friday's have fish fries in Wisconsin, but for an authentic one try American Serb Memorial Hall in Milwaukee (414.545.6030).

You won't find any ice cream in Wisconsin. It's frozen custard here—a rich, creamy, dense frozen dessert made with plenty of egg yolk and Wisconsin cream. Kopp's, Culver's, and Belt's soft serve duke it out for first place in cheesehead hearts. Of the three, Culver's has multiple locations and an impressive menu for a franchise. Culver's and Kopp's both serve another of the state's culinary passions: the butter burger. In some places, this sandwich is called a slider. It's a simple burger on a bun, but with a generous smear of Wisconsin butter that makes the burger so slick it slides right off the bun.

In Madison, hip, retro diners like Hubbard Avenue Diner (608.831.6800) and Monty's Blue Plate Special add more flair to casual comfort food than it's ever had. Being near the University of Wisconsin, these restaurants are as likely to serve vegetarian meatloaf as the real, meat-lover's variety, but the real test comes when the fork hits the pie. Thankfully, the sweets in Monty's Blue Plate Special's glass case pass the "homemade" test.

NORTHWEST

ANCHOR BAR

413 Tower Ave.
Superior, Wisconsin 54880
715.394.9747
www.anchorbar.freeservers.com

Lunch and dinner seven days a week 11 am–midnight

Hamburgers $1.75–$4.75

Cash, Full bar

The Anchor Bar is known for its burgers—which makes sense since they serve very little else. (The menu of four other sandwiches offers descriptions like "Ham sandwich: great if you like ham.") So how does a place become famous for its food with such a limited menu? According to manager Bean Prettie, Anchor Bar is one of the dying breed of neighborhood bars that people embrace. "It's a real small place," she says. "It's not fancy, it's no Applebee's."

But food lovers know what they like and that includes Anchor Bar's burgers. A bestseller is the cashew burger—a hand-formed pattie made of freshly ground beef, topped with cashews and Swiss cheese. But even Anchor Bar's menu wouldn't be complete without freshly cut french fries. "Do you cut those every morning?" I asked. "Oh, no," said Bean, horrified. "We cut them right when you order them. When you eat them they were cut just a few minutes ago."

EGG TOSS CAFÉ

41 Manypenny Ave.
Bayfield, Wisconsin 54814
715.779.5181
www.eggtoss-bayfield.com

May 1–December 31: Breakfast and lunch seven days a week 7 am–1 pm

$2.50–$8

MCC

The stellar breakfast menu ranges from traditional (the fisherman's platter features two eggs, two sausage links, two strips of bacon, hashbrowns, and toast) to the sublime: Crabby Benny is eggs benedict with crab cakes in place of Canadian bacon. French Ecstasy is an aptly named sandwich of sliced homemade cinnamon bread filled with cream cheese, dipped in batter, and cooked on a hot griddle.

Maggie's

257 Manypenny Ave.
Bayfield, Wisconsin 54814
715.779.5641
www.maggies-bayfield.com

Lunch and dinner seven days a week 11 am–10 pm

$3.50–$14

MCC

Maggie's is the kind of lunch and casual dinner place every town wishes it had. The restaurant offers solid renditions of American fare like Black Angus burgers, pizzas cooked in a stone-hearth oven, steamy-hot fajitas, and entrée salads. It's quirky and locally owned, and features seasonal delicacies like fresh herring in late winter and early spring.

Wild Rice

84860 Old San Rd.
Bayfield, Wisconsin 54814
715.779.9881
www.wildricerestaurant.com

June–September: Dinner Tuesday–Saturday 6 pm–10 pm. October and May: Dinner Thursday–Saturday 6 pm–9 pm. Closed Sunday and Monday. Closed November 1–first Thursday in May.

Ⓢ First courses $7.50–$14.50; Entrees $22–$36; Bar menu $3.50–$9.50

Ⓐ MCC, Full bar

ⓘ Reservations recommended for dining room. Bar is come as you are. Note the seasonal hours—be sure to call first.

This is the fine-dining anchor of restaurateur Mary H. Rice's restaurant group Flamingos Up North, based in the Bayfield area. The group includes two more casual restaurants worth visiting: the Egg Toss Café and Maggie's (listed on the two previous pages).

The building that houses Wild Rice is nothing short of spectacular. Designed for Rice by Duluth architect David Samela, the modern wood-frame restaurant features a glass and aluminum wine tower in the main entry with four hundred selections of wine (which earned the restaurant a Best of Award of Excellence from *Wine Spectator* in 2003).

The menu, like all good contemporary American restaurants today, is seasonal and inspired by local ingredients. Recent menu items include white asparagus in puff pastry with hollandaise sauce and horseradish-crusted venison rack with sweet potato gratin and caramelized onion-brandy glaze.

For those without deep pockets or reservations, the bar at Wild Rice is a pleasant alternative, featuring light fare such as creamy wild rice soup with roasted chicken and Granny Smith apples, and Alsatian tarte flambe with Nueske's bacon, crème fraiche, onion, and petite baby green salad.

E | East

Charcoal Inn

1313 S. Eighth St.
Sheboygan, Wisconsin 53081-5325

☎ 920.458.6988

🕘 Breakfast, lunch, and dinner Monday–Friday 6 am–9 pm, Saturday 6 am–7 pm. Closed Sunday.

Ⓢ $1.40–$4.20

★ Cash

! Second location—1637 Geele Ave., 920.458.1147

Like all great cuisines of the world, Sheboygan's intriguing culinary history lies in preparation techniques: Here, they cook everything over charcoal, including eggs.

Sheboygan restaurants also are known for hard rolls and bratwurst, especially the double brat: two bratwursts, split down the middle, grilled 'til they're spitting fat and popping loudly. The peppery, tangy brats at Charcoal Inn are forked onto a hard roll and, if you like, slathered with mustard or grilled onions or both. How could Sheboygan not be world-famous for this creation? How can anyone leave Sheboygan without trying it, knowing that this luxury is not duplicated elsewhere?

Later, in the kitchen at home, one can only dream about this sandwich. The broiler cannot do it justice, and despite its practical nature, it's easy to feel lukewarm about the gas grill. The ancient wisdom of charcoal speaks from deep inside the earth, where it is compressed by the forces of nature and will ultimately imbue sausages with a rousing flavor.

After the Charcoal Inn in Sheboygan, no bratwurst in its slick, hot glory will ever be the same. This is what you risk by eating here. But just like an art lover must visit the Louvre, you must open the laminated white menu at Charcoal Inn, wave off the smoke from your neighbor's ashtray, and double fist a double brat.

Kroll's West

1990 S. Ridge Rd.
Green Bay, Wisconsin 54304-4125
☎ 920.497.1111
www.krollswest.com

🕘 Lunch and dinner Sunday–Thursday 10:30 am–midnight, Friday and Saturday 10:30 am–1 am

$ Lunch $2.30–$7.50; Dinner $6.50–$10.75

★ MCC, Full bar

Located across from Lambeau field, home of the Green Bay Packers, this traditional restaurant cooks on charcoal grills and is famous for butter burgers (hamburgers served on a buttered roll) and bratwurst.

Schreiner's Restaurant

168 N. Pioneer Rd.
Fond du Lac, Wisconsin 54935
☎ 920.922.0590
www.fdlchowder.com

🕘 Breakfast, lunch, and dinner seven days a week 6:30 am–8:30 pm

$ Breakfast $5–$8; Lunch $7–$10; Dinner $7–$12

★ MCC, Full bar

After sixty years in the business, Schreiner's Restaurant is still a Sunday dinner kind of place. The atmosphere is comfortable and cozy, and the menu is reliable, with stewed chicken and dumplings on Tuesdays, roasted loin of pork on Wednesdays, and boneless short ribs of beef on Saturdays.

Schreiner's menu is so reliable, in fact, that only once has the Tuesday special been off the menu. "It was the Tuesday after a major holiday," remembers owner Paul Cunningham. "And we didn't have any chickens. After that day, with three hundred guests clamoring for their chicken and dumplings, I swore if it [a holiday on Monday] ever happened again I'd drive all the way to Green Bay to get the darn chickens!"

The chicken and dumplings are worth a little clamoring: three to four inches across, the tender, moist dumplings are cooked in rich chicken gravy and served with fall-apart tender chicken on the bone. Homemade baked goods like pecan rolls and rhubarb raspberry pie are also not to be missed.

White Gull Inn

4225 Main St.
Fish Creek, Wisconsin 54212
☎ 920.868.3517
www.whitegullinn.com

🕘 Breakfast, lunch, and dinner seven days a week. Breakfast 7:30 am–12 pm; Lunch 12 pm–2:30 pm. Seasonal candlelight dinner hours alternate with fish boil nights. Please call to verify schedule.

$ Breakfast and lunch $5–$10; Dinner first courses $5–$8; Entrees $21–$25; Fish boil $17.75 for adults, $10.75 for children

! MCC, Wine and beer

The White Gull Inn is a bed and breakfast with a restaurant open to the public. Popular fish boil nights are a Door County tradition, and they're done here with style: freshly caught white fish is cooked outside over a blazing wood fire, partnered with buttery new potatoes and cherry pie a la mode for dessert.

S | South

Bendtsen's Bakery

3200 Washington Ave.
Racine, Wisconsin 53405-3037
262.633.7449
www.bendtsensbakery.com

Monday–Saturday 5:30 am–5:30 pm. Closed Sunday.

$5.25–$7.00

MCC

Closed week after Easter

Bendtsen's Bakery has a little café offering coffee and espresso drinks to enjoy while you work your way through a kringle. In case you're thinking this Danish treat is a donut, a kringle weighs eighteen ounces and is split by at least two people. During hard times, an entire family can be satisfied by a single ring of this fabulous, buttery fried dough.

Coquette Café

316 N. Milwaukee St.
Milwaukee, Wisconsin 53202
414.291.2655
www.coquettecafe.com

Lunch and dinner Monday–Thursday 11 am–10 pm, Friday 11 am–11 pm, Saturday 5 pm–11 pm. Closed Sunday.

First courses $4.25–$10; Salads, sandwiches, and pizzas $4–$15.50; Entrees $10.75–$16

MCC, Full bar

Owned by restaurant pros Angela and Sanford D'Amato (See Sanford Restaurant, page 173), Coquette Café is a French-inspired bistro with peasant fare standards like French onion soup, snails in garlic-parsley butter, and coq au vin—chicken braised in red wine with pearl onions and mushrooms.

Culver's Custard

716 Phillips Blvd.
Sauk City, Wisconsin 53583
608.643.6620
www.culvers.com

Seven days a week 10 am–10 pm

$5–$7

MCC

Multiple locations; some take credit cards, some don't

Culver's has a big menu for a fast food chain, with Wisconsin flair: butter burgers are on the menu (a hamburger served on a toasted, buttered bun), plus fried cheese curds, pot roast, and chicken salad. The custard is thick and creamy, and shakes and malts are made to order with fresh fruit.

Elegant Farmer

1545 Main St.
Mukwonago, Wisconsin 53149
262.363.6770
www.elegantfarmer.com

Seven days a week 8 am–6 pm

$1.80–$10.50

MCC

Open longer hours during the summer

The Elegant Farmer is an elaborate farm stand with homemade breads, salads, pastries, and soups for carry out, in addition to fresh farm produce and house cider-cured hams. Picnic tables are set outside during warmer weather.

Ella's Deli & Ice Cream Parlor

2902 E. Washington Ave.
Madison, Wisconsin 53704-5143

☎ 608.241.5291

🕘 Breakfast, lunch, and dinner Sunday–Thursday 10 am–10 pm, Friday and Saturday 10 am–11 pm

$ $6–$10

★ MCC

Ella's Deli is a child's dream and a neurotic's nightmare. The restaurant features a brightly lit carousel outside that's operational in warm weather. Inside, the carnival continues with an interior design built around flashing, colorful, animated toys that hum and buzz and whir. For a six-year-old, Ella's is pure magic, but Woody Allen couldn't handle it for a New York minute.

The menu features kosher-style Jewish deli fare like corned beef sandwiches and deli salads, but many people make the journey with dessert in mind. The Number One is a dessert bestseller: a thick slice of homemade poundcake grilled to a caramelly crisp and topped with three scoops of homemade vanilla ice cream and hot fudge.

Jacobson Brothers Meats

3050 Cahill Main
Madison, Wisconsin 53711

☎ 608.273.2333

🕘 Monday–Friday 9 am–7 pm, Saturday 9 am–6 pm, Sunday 9 am–5 pm

$ $4–$6

★ MCC

! Carryout only

Jacobson Brothers Meats is known for its American-classic picnic fare: homemade American potato salad; coleslaw; and eight-layer salad with lettuce, celery, broccoli, onion, mayonnaise dressing, cheese, peas, and bacon. Other bestsellers include the shredded meat sandwiches—beef, turkey, and barbecue pork, plus Jacobson Brothers' hams.

Kewpee

520 Wisconsin Ave.
Racine, Wisconsin 53403-1051
262.634.9601
www.kewpee.com

Breakfast, lunch, and dinner Monday–Friday 7 am–6 pm, Saturday 7 am–5 pm. Closed Sunday.

Sandwiches $.90–$2.30

Cash

Racine's Kewpee diner is one of the last of the Kewpee franchises begun in the 1920s and popular throughout the Midwest. Here you'll find the food that made the chain popular: hand-formed burgers made of beef ground fresh every morning, homemade rootbeer, and shakes and malts.

The original building that housed Racine's Kewpee diner is long gone, but a new retro-looking diner is located in the same place. It's clean and bright, with a Kewpie doll collection on display and customized "Kewpee" tiles along the walls depicting a Kewpie doll in the restaurant's blue and white color scheme.

Kopp's Custard

5373 N. Port Washington Rd.
Glendale, Wisconsin 53217-4917
414.961.3288
www.kopps.com

Sunday–Thursday 10:30 am–11 pm, Friday and Saturday 10:30 am–11:30 pm

Custard $1.51–$4.75; Sandwiches $1.60–$4.55

MCC

Additional locations in Brookfield and Greenfield

You've got to love a frozen custard business that routinely makes gourmet custards so expensive to produce they're unprofitable to sell—including macadamia nut custard ("This is too expensive for us to make—so don't buy it!" the menu says) and double truffle (chocolate truffle-flavored custard with chocolate truffle pieces).

But even better is Kopp's Custard's dedication to its local baseball team, the Milwaukee Brewers. Always the flavor of the day on opening day, Kopp's "Pretzels and Beer" is root beer-flavored custard with white chocolate-covered pretzels.

Marigold Kitchen

118 S. Pinckney St.
Madison, Wisconsin 53703-3318
☎ 608.661.5559

🕘 Breakfast and lunch Monday–Friday 7 am–3 pm; Brunch Saturday 7 am–2 pm

$ Breakfast $5–$10; Brunch and lunch $6–$12

★ MCC, Full bar

! Order at the counter. Staff bring your food to you.

The Marigold Kitchen is a casual downtown eatery with a creative, gourmet menu. French toast is topped with pastry cream, almonds, and fresh berries. Soups are homemade and feature fresh herbs; try the cold tomato bread soup. Sandwiches star high-end ingredients, such as the grilled mahi mahi on ciabatta toast with lime mayonnaise and Asian sesame slaw.

Monty's Blue Plate Diner

2089 Atwood Ave.
Madison, Wisconsin 53704
☎ 608.244.8505
www.foodfightinc.com

🕘 Breakfast, lunch, and dinner Monday–Thursday 7 am–9 pm, Friday 7 am–10 pm Saturday 7:30 am–10 pm, Sunday 7:30 am–9 pm

$ $4–$10

★ MCC, Beer and wine

Monty's Blue Plate Diner is owned by the hipster restaurant group known as Food Fight Inc. The group has several winning restaurants around town, including Hubbard Avenue Diner (mentioned on page 158), that feature attractive interiors and with-it staff.

What's nice about Monty's is its range. While true to the comfort food "diner" image, Monty's Blue Plate also offers plenty of vegetarian goodies for the healthier eaters among us. Diner items range from a fried egg sandwich (and breakfast is available all day) to roast pork with spiced apples and apple cider gravy.

Vegetarian menu items are inspired by the canon of Mollie Katzen's Moosewood cookbooks. "Meatless loaf of the Gods" is made of shredded onion and carrot plus a hefty dose of sharp Wisconsin cheddar cheese and ginger-cashew gravy—and if you'd think that's not delicious, you'd be wrong. According to manager Kathy Brooks, it's a bestseller.

Peter Sciortino Bakery

1101 E. Brady St.
Milwaukee, Wisconsin 53202

☎ 414.272.4623

Ⓛ Tuesday–Saturday 7 am–5 pm, Sunday 7 am–1 pm. Closed Monday.

Ⓢ $1.50–$2

★ MCC

! Carry-out only. A few tables outside in summer.

Siblings Maria, Guiseppe, and Luigi Vella began working at the Peter Sciortino Bakery in their early teens. By the time the oldest Vella reached college, this precocious trio approached owner

Peter Sciortino with an offer to buy the business and continue its tradition of high-quality Italian breads, cookies, and cannoli. Thank goodness such righteous work can go on.

Italian and French loaves are braided and baked each night, sprinkled with poppy and sesame seeds and shaped in honor of the holiday of the moment: a cross for Easter, a heart for Valentine's Day. Italian cookies come in more than thirty-two varieties in a multitude of colors, some piped from pastry bags, others hand-rolled and cut. Likewise, the Vellas believe in making their cannolis the hard way. Each pastry shell is filled with sweetened ricotta cheese and miniature chocolate chips when ordered, so that the crisp pastry doesn't get soggy or moist. The ends of the cannoli are then decorated with glazed cherries, powdered sugar, and a shower of chopped pecans.

The Pine Cone

685 W. Linmar Lane
I-94 & Highway 26
Johnson Creek, Wisconsin 53038
920.699.2767

Open 24 hours seven days a week

$2.25–$12

MCC

This family-owned truck stop is a treasure trove of comfort food. A bakery near the entrance is loaded with pastries like caramel-pecan rolls, pies, bearclaws, and eclairs, plus gigantic candied apples.

The menu is built for big appetites. A hot roast beef sandwich comes with mashed potatoes and gravy, a cup of rich homemade chicken and dumplings soup, and a large dinner roll with butter.

You can sit at the counter and have a chat with the doting staff, or sit at one of the tables equipped with phones for professional drivers. The Pine Cone resonates with competent family-ownership: it's pleasant, clean, and well-lit, servers seem friendly and happy, and it's busy almost all the time.

Polonez

4016 S. Packard Ave.
Milwaukee, Wisconsin 53235-4834

414.482.0080

Lunch Tuesday–Friday 11 am–3 pm; Dinner Tuesday–Thursday and Saturday 5 pm–9 pm, Friday 4 pm–9 pm, Sunday 2 pm–8 pm; Brunch Sunday 11 am–2 pm

$5–$10

MCC

A Polish restaurant with one of the best Friday fish fries in town, Polonez's chef and co-owner (with wife Aleksandra) George Burzynski was named a "chef to watch" by restaurant critic Ann Christenson in *Milwaukee Magazine's* Best Dining issue in 2003. His recipes for pierogis, stuffed cabbage, and creamed herring came with him from the old country, which he left in 1980.

River Lane Inn

4313 W. River Lane
Brown Deer, Wisconsin 53223-2425

414.354.1995

Lunch Monday–Friday 11:30 am–2:30 pm; Dinner Monday–Saturday 5 pm–10 pm

First courses $5–$9; Entrees $18–$25

MCC, Full bar

Seafood gets the emphasis on this upscale bistro's menu. Arctic char is topped with fresh arugula and sun-dried tomatoes, and sea scallops are paired with sliced oranges. The dishes here are fresh and contemporary, and the dining room is filled with savvy diners.

Sanford Restaurant

1547 N. Jackson St.
Milwaukee, Wisconsin 53202-2001
414.276.9608
www.sanfordrestaurant.com

Dinner Monday–Thursday 5:30 pm–9 pm, Friday 5:30 pm–10 pm, Saturday 5 pm–10 pm

Prix fixe \$39–\$75; First courses \$7–\$17; Entrees \$24–\$29

MCC, Full bar

See Sanford's sister restaurant, Coquette Café (page 165), for more casual bistro fare.

A fine-dining bargain offering prix-fixe menus, chef-owned and operated Sanford Restaurant is named for Sanford D'Amato, a Culinary Institute of America graduate who's garnered almost every accolade in his field, including the James Beard award for best chef in the Midwest.

The menu is contemporary American, influenced by fresh, local, seasonal ingredients and French preparation techniques, the most elegant dishes being the likes of pomegranate molasses glazed squab with roasted figs.

The latest best thing about Sanford is its seasonal four-course menus. The price is a steal—\$39 for four courses, including such creative fare as leek waterzooi (a cream-based Belgian fish stew thickened with egg yolk) with sugar snap peas and bacon, and rhubarb tart with cranberry ice cream in spring.

Solly's Grille

4629 N. Port Washington Rd.
Milwaukee, Wisconsin 53212
414.332.8808

Breakfast, lunch, and dinner Tuesday–Saturday 6:30 am–8 pm

\$5–\$10

MCC

Since 1936, Solly's has made the definitive butter burgers, cheesehead burgers, and fresh banana malts.

Speed Queen

1130 W. Walnut St.
Milwaukee, Wisconsin 53205-1721
414.265.2900
www.foodspot.com/speedqueen

Lunch and dinner Monday–Thursday 11 am–12:30 am, Friday 11 am–3:30 am, Saturday 11 am–2 am. Closed Sunday.

$4–$16

Cash

Speed Queen thrives in this rough neighborhood because its barbecue demands respect. Saucy, hardwood-smoked pork shoulder is served on a soft white bun with a side of mustard-rich potato salad. You can also get fried perch in a crisp cornmeal crust, plus ribs, turkey, and chicken.

Taqueria Azteca

119 E. Oklahoma St.
Milwaukee, Wisconsin 53207-26265
414.486.9447

Lunch Tuesday–Friday 11 am–2:30 pm; Dinner Tuesday–Thursday 5 pm–10 pm, Friday and Saturday 4 pm–11 pm, Sunday 4 pm–8 pm; Brunch Sunday 11 am–4 pm

$5–$10

MCC, Full bar

Homemade salsa, interesting nightly quesadilla specials, live music on weekends, specialty margaritas—it's all here at this popular Mexican restaurant, plus friendly servers and a pleasant, family-friendly atmosphere.

Three Brothers's Restaurant

2414 S. St. Clair St.
Milwaukee, Wisconsin 53207-1928
414.481.7530

Dinner Tuesday–Thursday 5 pm–10 pm, Saturday 4 pm–11 pm, Sunday 4 pm–10 pm. Closed Mondays.

$5–$15

Cash

Reservations required

This Serbian restaurant is located in a turn-of-the-century tavern and serves roast lamb, goulash, veal, and burek, a light pastry filled with meat or cheese.

Unique Café

1100 Wisconsin Ave.
Boscobel, Wisconsin 53805
608.375.4465

Breakfast and lunch Monday–Friday 6 am–7 pm, Saturday 6 am–4 pm, Sunday 6 am–2 pm

$2–$6

Cash

Unique Café's coffee club comes in for a cup of coffee and cookies twice a day, but there's no need to visit this small town café so often, especially if you indulge in "Doyle's concoction." According to Karmen, a staffer here, Doyle's concoction (named after the owner) "weighs about three pounds, I swear! It's a six-egg omelet stuffed with corned beef, Swiss cheese, hash browns, and cheddar cheese." Room for dessert? Get a slice of sour cream raisin pie. The kitchen staff at Unique Café make about four different kinds of pie a day.

Watt's Tea Shop

761 N. Jefferson St.
Milwaukee, Wisconsin 53202-3707
414.291.5120

Breakfast, lunch, and tea Monday–Saturday
9 am–4 pm

$5–$10

MCC

This old-fashioned, prim tea shop is located in the George Watt's China Shop. Specialties include the filled sunshine cake (a layer cake with boiled frosting), cream of tomato and basil soup, ginger toast, and finger sandwiches.

W | West

Bogus Creek Café and Bakery

114 Spring St.
Stockholm, Wisconsin 54769
715.442.5017

Memorial Day–November: Breakfast and lunch seven days a week 9 am–5 pm. Call to confirm hours in off-season.

$6–$15

Cash, Wine and beer

Bogus Creek's motto is "our food is real," meaning real freshly baked breads, breakfast items like crisp Belgian waffles, and specialty sausages like a bratwurst stuffed with pork and wild rice, plus micro-brewed beer. All this is served to guests seated on a real pretty garden patio (or inside the dining room, if you choose).

Norske Nook

13804 7th St.
Osseo, Wisconsin 54758
715.597.3688
www.norskenook.com

Breakfast, lunch, and dinner seven days a week 5:30 am–8 pm. Extended summer hours.

Breakfast $3–$7.20; Lunch and dinner $4–$13

MCC

Multiple locations

This Norwegian restaurant steals your heart with its earnest presentation of lovely comfort food. An entire, separate menu is dedicated to lefse. The deprived may not know the glories of lefse—a

Norwegian flatbread shaped like a thin white disk similar to a flour tortilla. But honestly, tortillas can't hold a candle to lefse, which is thicker and with a delightful flavor derived from its key ingredients—baked russet potatoes, cream, and butter.

Norske Nook also features twenty-eight kinds of made-from-scratch pie—including blackberry cream cheese pie (why isn't this available everywhere pie is sold in America? Is there no justice?) and National Pie Championship first place winner 2003—the banana cream pie. The critics have spoken: banana cream pie does not get any better than this. You'll also find comfort food classic entrees like Swiss steak, Swedish meatballs, and creamed chicken over biscuits.

C | Central

Belt's Soft Serve

2140 Division St.
Stevens Point, Wisconsin 54481
715.344.0049

Seven days a week 11 am–10 pm

$1.10–$3.85

Cash

Many a frozen custard stand serves blended treats with packaged candy like M&M's and Snicker's bars. But how many places do you know that bake their own brownies and mix their own cookie dough for such frozen concoctions? Such labor for the sake of pure pleasure is the height of purpose at Belt's Soft Serve.

This seasonal ice cream shop is so pleasing, in fact, that when Belt's opens in early March, customers camp out in the parking lot to be first in line. The gild on the lily here is size: Belt's flurries are big and bigger. Belt's also makes its own drumsticks and turtle bars. It's all love.

Guide to Restaurants

Geographical listing of Restaurants

Illinois

Northwest

Northeast

Southeast

Southwest

Central

Indiana

Northwest

North

Northeast

East

Southeast

Southwest

West

Central

Iowa

Northwest

Northeast

Southeast

Southwest

Central

Kentucky

Northwest

Central

Wisconsin

Northwest

East

South

West

Central

About the Author

Dawn Simonds grew up in Ohio, hiding out in her mother's garden munching sugar snap peas off the vine before dinner. She ate her way through Italy, Mexico, and Chile before settling in Cincinnati, where she is the restaurant critic for *Cincinnati* magazine. She lives with her husband and two children.

Everybody Loves Ice Cream
by Shannon Jackson Arnold

Three scoops please: a travel book, a cookbook, and a pop culture history all in one, the most complete treatment of the subject a reader can find anywhere. Whether you're looking for a great ice cream stand nearby, a recipe for rocky road, or an explanation for what makes an ice cream "super-premium," you'll find it here. It's true that *Everybody Loves Ice Cream,* and this book tells you why.

Packed with photos and designed with mix-ins and toppings of all sorts, this charming book is like a trip to the soda fountain—something everybody enjoys. Author Shannon Jackson Arnold covers everything from a factory tour to homemade recipes, from definitions for various frozen desserts to soda jerk jargon.

Everybody Loves Ice Cream provides readers with a parfait look at every aspect of our favorite frozen treat:

- what's the best and where to get it, across the country
- how to make delicious ice cream yourself
- how the manufacturers make it
- where and how it was invented and how it has evolved
- how it has played a part in American culture

Step right up for a taste of the sweetest book ever!

Shannon Jackson Arnold is a freelance writer and editor living in Milwaukee, Wisconsin. Her work appears in many magazines, including *Marie Clare* and *Wisconsin Trails,* and she is the former editor of *Ohio* magazine.

Price: $19.99 Paperback, 4-color throughout, 8 ¾ x 8 ¾
ISBN: 1-57860-165-7

Books of Interest

Corn Country: Celebrating Indiana's Favorite Crop
by Sam Stall

Corn is king! As far as the eye can see, as fragrant as summer, visions of cornfields wrap around our senses like a silky husk on a fresh ear of golden kernels. Corn is big business as well, harvested on half of the state's 12 million available agricultural acres. Simply, no other state loves corn the way Hoosiers do. In *Corn Country,* author Sam Stall and photographer Darryl Jones delight readers with their verbal and visual chronicle of Indiana's love affair with its favorite crop.

Stall's narrative captures a year in the life of corn, from tilling to planting to harvesting; in tandem with Jones' eloquent photos, he has chronicled the heart and spirit of Midwest heritage.

Complete with history, recipes, testimonials and photos that capture the spirit of Indiana, *Corn Country* highlights the way corn has shaped Indiana since before there was an Indiana to the present day. Corn festivals, corn advertising memorabilia, farmers, collectors and corn enthusiasts round out this fascinating and endearing tribute to everyone who's ever enjoyed a buttery sweet cob or a handful of popcorn at the movies.

Sam Stall, a native Hoosier, is a freelance journalist and the former editor of *Indianapolis Monthly* magazine. Sam and his wife live in Indianapolis.

Darryl Jones, a freelance photographer since 1975, has spent most of his adult life documenting the beauty and character of Indiana's landscapes and people. He lives on a small farm in Owen County, Indiana.

Price: $23.99 Paperback
ISBN: 1-57860-118-5

To order call: 1(800) 343-4499 www.emmisbooks.com
EMMIS BOOKS 1700 MADISON ROAD CINCINNATI, OHIO 45206

Tray Chic: Celebrating Indiana's Cafeteria Culture

by Sam Stall

While saying "cafeteria" in most parts of the country is an invitation to antacid therapy and a bus ride out of town, say "cafeteria" in the Midwest (and in Indiana, especially) and people will smile and say, "Let's eat!"

Why is it that here in the breadbasket of the United States, a surprising number of family-owned cafeteria businesses thrive and continue to expand? Why do the fresh foods, savory meats, and rainbows of Jell-O still beckon to legions of appreciative diners here and nowhere else? How can these landmark eateries, where it's not uncommon to see lines stretched out the door, successfully compete with high-concept theme restaurants, all-you-can-eat chains, and even fast-food?

It's the personal, hands-on, and some would even say down-home approach that works: A commitment to the customer. Some Hoosier cafeterias even serve as many as two hundred food items every day. In *Tray Chic,* Sam Stall lovingly tells the stories of this cafeteria culture, dotes on beloved house specialties, and collects photos and memorabilia that recall a time gone by.

Sam Stall is a freelance journalist and the former editor of *Indianapolis Monthly.* He is the author of *Special Delivery,* the story of America's first sextuplets, and the co-author of *As Seen on TV: 50 Amazing Products and the Commercials That Made Them Famous.* He lives in Indianapolis with his wife, Jami.

Price: $22.99 Paperback (4-color throughout)
ISBN: 1-57860-136-3

To order call: 1(800) 343-4499 www.emmisbooks.com
EMMIS BOOKS 1700 MADISON ROAD CINCINNATI, OHIO 45206